MODELLING AND PAINTING

World War I Allied Figures

MODELLING AND PAINTING

World War I Allied Figures

Mike Butler

THE CROWOOD PRESS

First published in 2022 by
The Crowood Press Ltd
Ramsbury, Marlborough
Wiltshire SN8 2HR

enquiries@crowood.com

www.crowood.com

British Library Cataloguing-in-Publication Data
A catalogue record for this book is available from the British Library.

ISBN 978 0 7198 4092 0

Frontispiece
My painted version of Captain Philip Henry Fry at Gallipoli, ready to add to a custom base. This is an original one-off by sculptor Phil Walden.

Typeset by Chennai Publishing Services
Cover design by Blue Sunflower Creative
Printed and bound in India by Parksons Graphics

Contents

Dedication

This book is dedicated to my family's forebears who served in World War I: some returned, some did not.

The following is our family roll of honour:

4/1153 Sapper **Donald Eddie**, NZ Engineers. Died as a prisoner of war on 23 February 1917 in Lille, France. Twenty-four years old.

16021 Private **Arthur Wilks**, 1st Battalion, Otago Infantry Regiment. Killed in action on 7 June 1917 in Messines, Belgium. Twenty-three years old.

11/1314 Trooper (later Private) **Frederick (Fred) Francis**. Wellington Mounted Rifles and 2nd Battalion, Wellington Infantry Regiment. Killed in action on 31 July 1917 at La Basseville, France. Thirty-three years old.

11/1315 Trooper (later Driver) **Walter (Watt) Francis**. Wellington Mounted Rifles and NZ Field Artillery, Ammunition Column. Wounded in action on 29 May 1917 at Messines, France.

10/3656 Private **Percy Munn**, 2nd Battalion, Wellington Infantry Regiment. Wounded in action (three times on the Western Front).

6/630 Lance Corporal **Edward Flaherty**, 1st Battalion Canterbury Infantry Regiment. Wounded in action (twice at Gallipoli and once on the Western Front).

39067 Rifleman **Louis Xavier Le Vaillant**, 4th Battalion, NZ Rifle Brigade. Died of sickness. Forty-two years old.

70631 Trooper **Henry Christopher Moore**, Auckland Mounted Rifles. Medical discharge due to illness (diphtheria) contracted on active service.

13/2386 Trooper **Alfred Williscroft**, Auckland Mounted Rifles.

Donald.

PTE. A. J. WILKS,
of Purangi,
Killed in action.

TPR. F. W. (FRED) FRANCIS, of Pahiatua.
Killed in action.

GNR. W. FRANCIS,
of Palmerston North.
Wounded.

Arthur, Fred, Watt.

Percy.

Preface

Although I have been involved in military modelling and painting figures for many years, World War I is a recent focus brought about by a desire to recognize my New Zealand military ancestors. I was inspired to concentrate on this conflict when I was fortunate enough to have my name drawn in a ballot to attend the 2015 ANZAC Centennial Commemoration at Gallipoli in Turkey.

Atop Chunuk Bair, with my son Matthew beside New Zealand's memorial; the ground was captured and held by Lt Col Malone's men against massive odds in early August 1915.

Included in this book are illustrated plates drawn by my son Edward Butler. They are done in the style made famous by Bryan Fosten (aka 'Stan Catchpol') and Bill Donnelly in *Military Modelling* magazine in the 1980s and 1990s. These show the sequence of steps to applying a particular technique. Do use these to help increase your confidence in converting, sculpting and painting your World War I projects.

Also included are photographs of figures by my mentors, and many of my own finished projects, each with notes to help you study photographic detail more closely. I trust this book will become a valuable reference for those who model the Allied Nations of World War I.

I welcome feedback and questions on my techniques. Feel free to contact me by email: mikesuzb@gmail.com; or support me on Patreon www.patreon.com/MikeTheKiwi; or online at www.PlanetFigure.com, or www.facebook.com/michaeljbutlerNZ

Acknowledgements

As I work isolated from the wider modelling community I rely upon and am indebted to many people around the world who have helped me produce this book.

From the UK: Steve Warrilow, Steve Leadley, Mike Everest and Mike South of the 10th Essex Living History Group, Andy Robertshaw, Robin Buckland, Faris Siwadi for Poilu 'Olivères Collection' photos, Bryan Fosten (*aka* Stan Catchpol) RIP.

Tommy's War fans: Darren Parker Mead, Andy Belsey, Craig Hedgecock.

From the US: Paul Ondeck, Mike Good and Tim Farrell of ModelCellar; Albert Steiner.

From Europe: Edgar Liepinsh and Slava Krylov of Copper State Models.

From France: Jean-Luc Frey and Benoit Cauchies of Wars and Peaces, Philippe Martin, Chris Mills.

From Belgium: Henk Devos, David Moortgat for the Belgian background and photos.

From Portugal: Paulo Liberato.

From Australia: Phil Walden, Chris Roberts, Graham McNamara, Jim Shivers, Alan Mackie, Rob Wellington, Tony Dawe.

From Canada: John Aitken.

From South Korea: Young Bok Song, Man Jin Kim.

From Ireland: Keith Donnelly.

From Italy: Maurizio Fenucci, Maurizio Berselli, Fabrizio Marini.

From New Zealand: Iain Davidson, John Belcher, Andy Cairns, Aaron Fox, Mike Bourke, Mike Leet, Mark Dunsmuir, Barry O'Sullivan, Malcolm Thomas.

From Mr Black Publications in Greece: Stelios Demiras.

From Wingnut Wings Fans family: Richard Alexander, Francisco Guedes, David Wilson, Michael Scarborough.

From Asia: Yannick Olivères, Miles Humphreys, Scott Edwards.

And finally my family: without their love and patience I would not have achieved what I have. Suzanne, Edward and Matthew – my reason for being...

New Zealand memorial commemorating those who fell in or near Messines in 1917 and 1918, who have no known grave site; these include Arthur Wilks and Fred Francis. PHILIPPE MARTIN

Introduction

WORLD WAR I AND ANZACS...

With the centennial of World War I there has been a renewed interest in the 'War to End All Wars'. As part of this nostalgic look back a wide range of miniatures has been released for those who want to understand the technology, including that of armoured cars, aircraft and tanks.

This was a war that saw the development of technologies that would later influence society more broadly, especially in medical treatment and post-operative care. Aircraft, armoured vehicles, submarines and chemical warfare were used on a scale so devastating that it influenced all other conflicts that followed. It would also see the beginning of the end for cavalry and the large-scale use of animals in logistics.

Accounts of this momentous upheaval were shared widely, in letters sent home by the troops themselves, or more officially by a handful of war correspondents, who helped shape the narrative during and after the war. This latter group established some of the myths of World War I, with reporting heavily biased to the experience of their own countrymen. This was reinforced by soldiers, nurses, airmen and sailors who dispelled the myths of a glorious war with the honest realities of the impact it had on them. New Zealand alone sent 42 per cent of its eligible males. Together with Australia, India, Canada and South Africa, almost two million enlisted to fight. These men and women were critical in bolstering the European Allies – France, Britain, Belgium, Russia, Italy, the United States, Japan and Portugal.

Over time, tales of the war were depicted in books, films, music and television, all adding their own interpretation. Some of the most profound depictions became the defining record of the war, such as Remarque's *All Quiet on the Western Front* (also known as *Nothing New on the Western Front*) and Junger's *Storm of Steel*, both seen from the perspective of the common German infantryman. On the Allied side, Vera Brittain, Rupert Brooke, Siegfried Sassoon, Wilfred Owen and Rudyard Kipling all wrote from intimate experience of the war. In Kipling's case he wrote about the death of his son, John Kipling, at only eighteen, in 1915 at Loos. Rudyard had lobbied to get his son 'Jack' a commission in the Guards, despite poor eyesight. This event summed up the sense of loss experienced by too many.

'Down under' in New Zealand and Australia a legend was being born, fashioned by newly commissioned reporter Captain (the Hon.) Charles Bean, along with fellow journalists Keith Murdoch and Malcolm Ross. The ANZACs were a military unit composed of Australian and New Zealand troops readied for the Gallipoli invasion. The date of this attack, 25 April 1915, was to become the commemorative milestone where future generations would gather to remember the sacrifices made in that war, and all wars since.

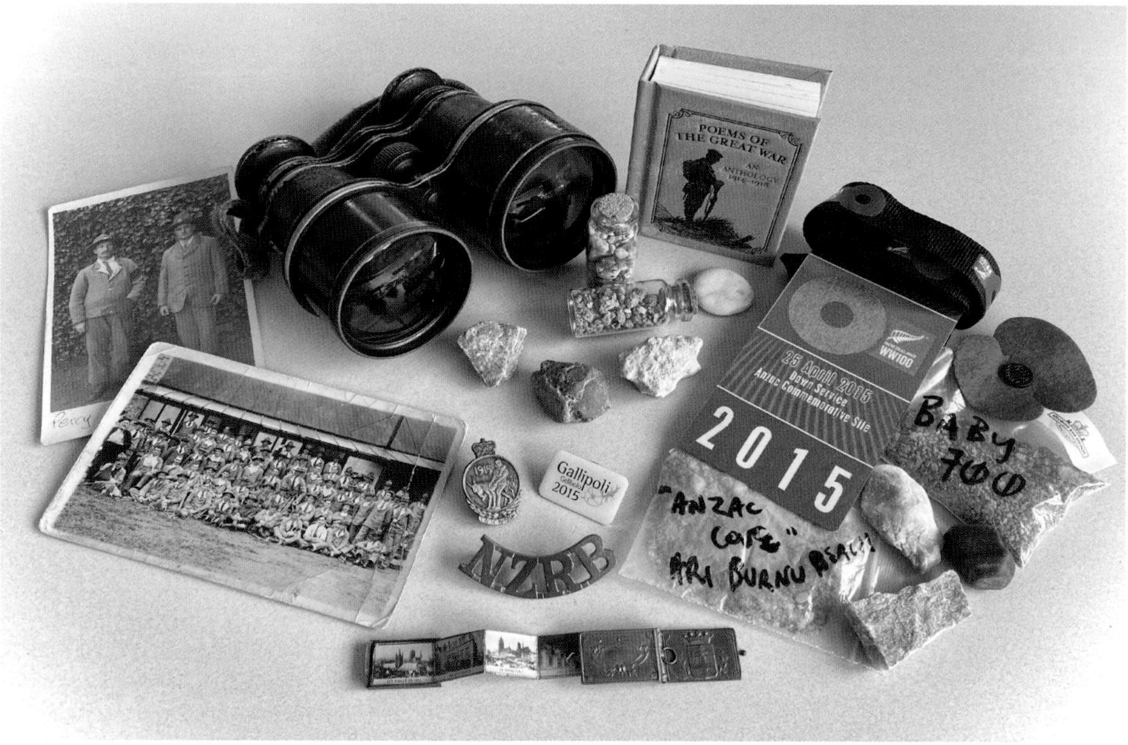

Family memorabilia connect today with then, such as binoculars donated to the war effort, a locket from Ypres, and Gallipoli souvenirs.

WHAT WORLD WAR I SOLDIERS LOOKED LIKE

An important first step in modelling World War I is to consider the subjects to recreate. Who were they, and what did they look like? When did they serve, and where? Books and photographs are normally the place to begin for inspiration, techniques and accurate information, particularly those books with illustrations of the look and feel of soldiers in their surroundings (*see* Appendix 2). However, there are other options worthy of note for research: postcards, art, movies, television, and, most helpful today, the work done by enthusiastic amateur historians who make and restore period costumes.

World War I pioneered war photography and film on a scale not seen before. These still and moving images were shared with audiences at home hungry for news of their loved ones. A common way for soldiers to stay in touch was through postcards from the front. These featured photographs of individuals, and also battlefront scenes that gave a glimpse of what was happening. Whilst many of these postcards, photographs and films were in black and white or sepia tone, they are part of a renaissance with the new technology of colouration. This is being done by professional artists, as well as hobbyists, and provides good painting references. However, caution is advised as each plate is only as good as the research done before the painstaking process of colouring begins.

A good example of colouration is the work by New Zealander Sir Peter Jackson and the teams at Wingnut Films and Weta Digital. They coloured hundreds of high-quality photographs from NZ Archives for their museum display in the Great War Exhibition. They then went on to produce the critically acclaimed film *They Shall Not Grow Old,*

The forgotten cost of war: a postcard depicting wounded ANZACs recovering in England in 1918. Percy Munn is second from the left seated on the ground. SOURCE: Postcard from the author's family.

coloured from many hours of Imperial War Museum archive footage. This is a definite watch for all World War I modellers.

Art painted or sculpted during and after World War I began to catalogue the look of those that fought, as well as the environments they fought in. The more realistic of these convey what it was like, as well as capturing a contemporary account suitable for modellers. The following are of particular note for study:

* The large-scale painting by ex-pat American John Singer Sargent, *Gassed*. It was reproduced in miniature form by Nino Pizzichemi for *Tommy's War*, to memorialize the effects of this horrific weapon and to raise funds for the Blind Veterans Association.
* The sketches and illustrations of Italian artist Fortunino Matania, which show real understanding of trauma, drama and action in battle. He was known to do his own research, visiting the trenches many times, as well as interviewing those who had been part of the action he depicted. His prolific output is full of vignette and diorama ideas, particularly of Allied operations. He said: 'Photography has made such great strides, so I turned to something else: the reconstruction of historical events.'

Another artist whose work deserves consideration by miniaturists is decorated World War I veteran Lt Charles Sergeant Jagger, MC. After serving in Gallipoli and on the Western Front, Jagger was commissioned as an official war artist. His first-hand education as a soldier, where he was wounded in action three times, comes across in each of his large-scale sculptures. Well-known modern UK miniature sculptor, Carl Reid, has reproduced some of these for ModelCellar and other brands.

Films and later television programmes can provide useful information for the World War I modeller. However, it is important to be selective as these can confuse fiction with non-fiction, and plot lines often based on history can become loose when reproducing uniforms and equipment. Therefore do check before you copy. Notable examples worth using as reference for ideas are the following:

* British: *Wings, Journey's End, 1917, The Trench, Testament of Youth, My Boy Jack*
* French: *Paths of Glory, La Grande Illusion*
* Canada and US: *Passchendaele, The Lost Battalion*
* ANZAC: *The Lighthorsemen, Gallipoli* (two items – a Peter Weir film and a Tolga Oren

documentary), *Beneath Hill 60, 25 April, ANZACs, Chunuk Bair, Charles Bean's Great War, Field Punishment No 1*

In more recent years a small number of re-enactment groups have been set up by enthusiasts to share their interests in a living history context. Considerable effort is taken by them to portray the World War I soldier, as well as explain how their equipment looked and functioned. The internet spreads this knowledge more extensively with online articles, images and videos. As a result these have become one of the most readily accessible research sources available. Using these resources for miniature projects is useful, however they should be cross-checked with period photos to ensure accuracy.

Groups that focus solely on World War I do tend to give a deeper purpose for this era, aiming to 'get it right'. One such group is 10th Essex, based in England, who specialize in representing Great War Tommies. Photographs taken with their kind support have been used in this book to explain and show uniform details.

The following are other historical reconstruction organizations meriting further investigation:

All Allies:

* Great War Association – www.greatwarassociation.com: an international body featuring a wide range of units from across the globe
* Reenactor Network – www.reenactor.net

UK: The 10th Essex Living History – www.10thessex.uk
Belgium: De Patrouilleurs – www.facebook.com/DePatrouilleurs
New Zealand: Historical Reenactment Society – www.hrs.org.nz

The following photographs show uniform details of the British soldier reconstructed.

A British Tommy enjoys a joke and a brew from an enamel mug. Tucked in his webbing is a set of wire cutters. SOURCE: Reconstruction of the British infantryman's uniforms courtesy of Mike Everest and Mike South of the 10th Essex Living History Group.

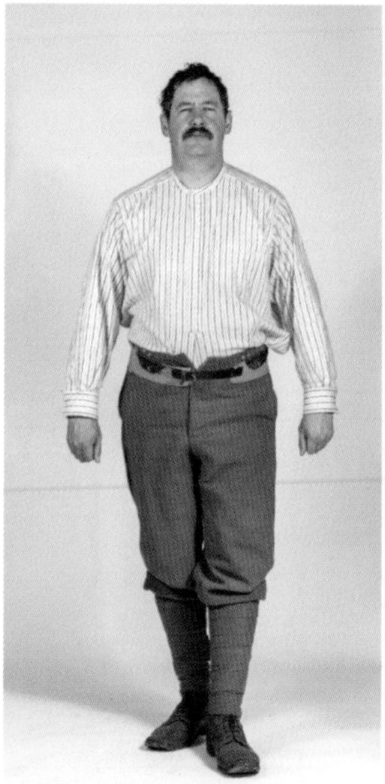

British undress clothing with a collarless, pin-striped shirt. Shirt colours varied from white through to light grey and light blue.

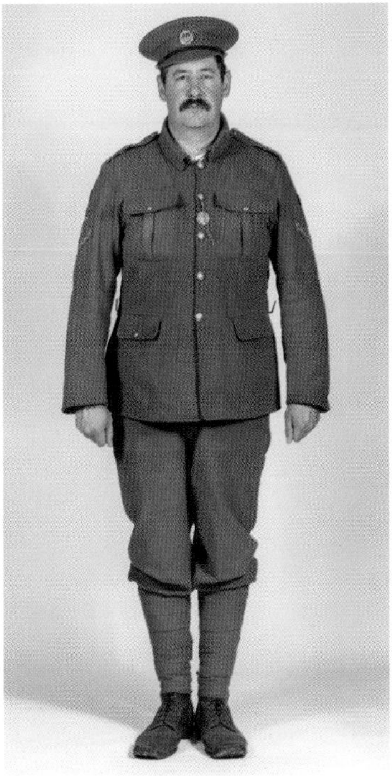

Service caps were worn in the early stages of war, then off duty. The small silver medallion is an army temperance medal for non-drinkers.

This 10th Essex lance corporal, a qualified PTI, uses his entrenching tool to dig a shell scrape. A cloth ration bag is tied to his back.

A figure kneeling or lying down cutting wire would be an interesting project, as poses such as this are rarely depicted in miniature.

1908 webbing, modified in 1914 when securing straps were added to the bottom pouches on the left side, also the detail on the cloth, .303 ammunition bandolier labelling.

This Tommy is prepared for hand-to-hand trench fighting with his bayonet unsheathed and his entrenching handle at the ready.

A classic grenade-throwing pose, helpful in showing how clothing, rifle and equipment sit in this extreme position.

This soldier, waiting to go over the top, has rolled up sandbags tucked behind his webbing pouches, ready to be filled when a trench is taken. SOURCE: Reconstruction of life in the trenches from Andy Belsey and Robin Buckland's photos of Andy Robertshaw's '24 Hour Trench' living history display.

A sergeant, bayonet fixed, crouches below the parapet in an authentic-looking trench line full of detail for adding to vignettes and dioramas.

A casually posed Lewis gunner has popped his pistol into his open gas-mask satchel should his MG jam or if he is out of ammunition.

The soldier's back view showing his damaged battle-jerkin leather, his entrenching tool muddied after being used as a seat, and elbows dirty after resting on them to aim his rifle.

Chapter One

Figure Kits

Model figures, busts and accessories come in a variety of forms; this chapter describes the choices available.

WHITE-METAL FIGURES AND BUSTS

White metal was used as the base material for the original toy soldiers, popular with children from Victorian times. Model figure kits made out of this metal began to appear post-World War II. Modellers liked this material because it gave the figure or bust an attractive, solid, natural weight. The sophistication of kits and sculpting gradually improved from the 1980s, and reached a peak in the early 2000s, with manufacturers such as France's Metal Modèles, who produce an attractive range of classically posed World War I figures covering all nations.

For World War I modellers the Scale Link brand from the 1980s was well known for its comprehensive 1:32 range. Their catalogue still boasts the broadest selection of figures, animals, equipment, artillery and spare accessories, representing almost all protagonists. There are still some important kits to be found, especially scenic items that can be used to supplement 1:32 figures and dioramas.

Steve Warrilow was an important pioneer in white-metal World War I figures with 'The Fusilier' range. Over almost three decades Steve sculpted and marketed his figures in the bigger scale of 75/80mm (1:24). Each model was uniquely styled, and had a feel for the common soldier. These kits are still eagerly sought today by modellers who crave the challenge of working with more robust white-metal figures.

Wargaming figures need to be durable, so were most commonly made in white metal, although some are coming out as injection-moulded plastic figures today. They are smaller in scale than kitsets, ranging from a tiny 1:285 through to 1:76 (also scaled in sizes 15mm, 25mm and 30mm). The correct proportions can be difficult to paint or sculpt due to this reduced size. They are, however, ideal for large-scale layouts, such as trench or attack scenes, where a number of figures can convincingly be painted up and displayed in a diorama to give a broader view of a scene.

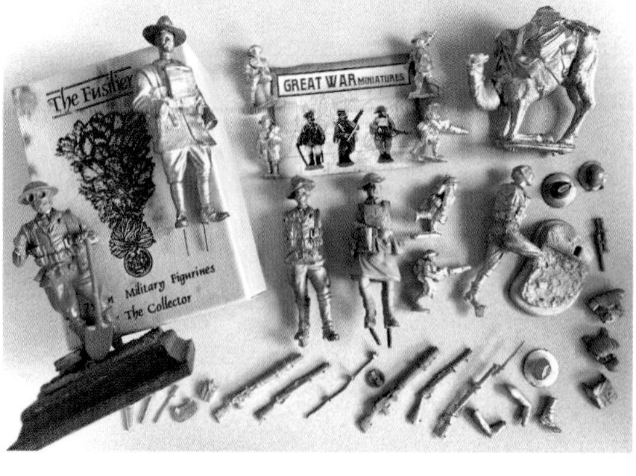

A selection of metal figures, out of production from The Fusilier and Thistle Miniatures, plus in production from Benieto and Great War.

INJECTION-MOULDED PLASTIC KITS

Plastic kitsets are manufactured by large companies that also produce armour, soft skin and aircraft model kits. Therefore they are normally produced in scales common to these companion products, either 1:72, 1:48, 1:35, 1:32, 1:24 or 1:16. Due to being mass-produced, they are typically cheaper, though this can also indicate the quality of the kit. Injection-moulded plastic is softer in detail, and therefore this detail requires sharpening. They are very good for beginners to learn on, and more advanced modellers can also get satisfactory results with extra attention. More recent kits are improving with state-of-the-art technology, making the most of 3D computer-aided design. The true potential of these kits can be further realized as donor figures for conversions with new heads, hands, equipment and detail added from scratch or spares.

Engineered plastic kit figures compared with resin kits, which are mostly handcrafted like AC Models diorama, though 3D sculpting and printing is growing.

RESIN FIGURE KITS AND BUSTS

Resin kits began to appear in the late twentieth century. They were made in rubber moulds, and were relatively inexpensive to produce. These were popularized by Belgian master modeller François Verlinden in the 1980–2000s, and have become the most preferred material for figure kits today. The material allows for high-quality, sharp definition in the mould-making process. A skilled caster can more easily replicate the exact precision of the sculptor's master figure. The only downside is that this fine detail can be fragile, especially if the resin is not left to cure fully, or moulds have begun to wear out. It is also the material of choice for forgers, because of its availability and reasonable ease of production.

Verlinden pioneered the superior final quality and lighter weight of resin, compared with white metal, as an ideal material to produce busts and 'SuperScale' (1:16) figures. This built a new market, which is now an important part of World War I figure modelling. These upsized figures and busts allow for more personal, individual studies and are a real challenge for the modeller who must find techniques suitable for closer examination.

PIRATES! A WORD OF WARNING ABOUT PIRACY AND FORGERY...

One of the biggest threats facing this hobby is that of piracy. This is where illegal copies are produced from original retail figures, which are used as cheap masters, to make an inferior product at a lower price. The price could be one of the reasons people choose to purchase these from online auction and trading sites. Another reason is that out-of-production or limited-run kits may be difficult to obtain. Typically these forged kits do not have correct packaging, if any, and are sold as basic kits, cast in resin with limited detail about the actual maker. Although original box art may have been used to advertise the copies on the trading

(Continued)

Continued

website, this is often not supplied and just used to lure unsuspecting purchasers. Unfortunately every pirated product that is purchased impacts on the returns made by the small niche manufacturers in the industry.

For truly authentic, good-quality figures and kits, always purchase directly from the maker, or a reputable reseller – a selection of these has been included in Appendix 1. If in any doubt, do reach out to trusted modellers in PlanetFigure or similar online forums to check on the authenticity of the reseller and their sales history.

One possible solution to piracy is the creation of commercial digital licences, where copies can be controlled by the sculptor, ensuring that only those who are official licensed rights holders can digitally print the figure. There will be many more developments over the years as 3D sculpting and printing continue to evolve.

Scratch-built figures need to be acknowledged as the premier form of model figure art. This is where an original concept is crafted out of odds and ends, often putty over a wire armature. While some modellers do not create entirely custom-made, or one-off figures, the same techniques can be used to convert or adapt existing kits. These are known as conversions. By making the most of commercial and hand-crafted parts, an original figure is possible. There is a wide array of accessories sets produced specifically for this purpose. These are aimed at the more difficult figure items such as heads, hands and weapons. The most highly regarded range are the Hornet headsets crafted by Roger Saunders in the most favoured modeller scales of 1:35 and 1:32. All modellers should invest in a few of these to help enhance plastic, metal, resin or scratch figures.

3D technology is the most exciting development of the twenty-first century for figure modellers. It undoubtedly lifts the bar for sculptors and provides an ever-growing range of new products to tempt figure modellers. These figures are sculpted using software programmes such as ZBrush. They can then be printed directly from a downloadable file to a 3D printer by the modeller, or by a manufacturer, who then casts resin figures for sale.

Chapter Two

Materials and Tools

PUTTY AND CLAYS

Putties and clays are a must for modelling figures and busts of all types. A wide variety of brands is available, and like paints, it is worth exploring what each can offer. They are magical materials used for filling gaps, masking and holding parts, and also creating and shaping parts. The main types and uses for modelling putties and clays are as follows:

Epoxy putty: This comes in two-part pots or rolls (Milliput), an A and a B part. One part is a resin, the other a hardener, and when blended together a chemical reaction occurs. The mixed parts naturally cure in the open air. This two-part epoxy putty is a multipurpose friend of the modeller. It can fill small gaps, build thin or thick layers, create flexible items such as straps, and is the base material of many hand-sculpted figures. It can be shaped, textured and smoothed, using a hand lotion or Nivea cream without needing further sanding.

Mixing different brands of epoxy putty will give blended properties from the individual parts. For example, varying proportions of a softer, malleable type (Duro or Green Stuff) combined with a firmer, hard-drying type (A&B, Apoxie or Magic Sculpt, Procreate) will yield different properties that are dissimilar from the original epoxy types.

Fillers: Single-mix modelling putty (AK, Squadron Signal, Tamiya, Humbrol) is generally supplied in tubes and can be acrylic or solvent-based. It is applied directly from the tube, with toothpicks or a rubber brush to fill gaps and add mild texture. It dries quickly and can be smoothed after drying, by sanding.

Polymer clay: This clay comes in an air-drying type (Das) that is smoothed with water and is useful for groundwork or bulk sculpting. The more common oven-baked version gives endless working time, making it ideal for simpler, more repetitive work such as sandbag walls or for complex art such as busts or full figures. To add to its versatility, oven-baked clay comes in plain-coloured professional sculptor packs (Sculpey, Beesputty) or artistic-coloured smaller units (Fimo, Cernit Du-Kit). For military modelling, regardless of which is used to create accessories or figures, once cured, all are treated as a painting surface just like any other material.

TIP

Use Blu Tack or Green Tack putty to remove fine lint, hair or objects from painted figures without damaging fragile surfaces.

TOOLS

Visibility aids are a valuable addition to any modeller's toolkit, regardless of how good your eyesight

This working tray contains tools and putties most commonly used for preparing figures and includes glues, shapers and magnifier glasses.

might be. These will help you to see the smallest features of a figure, plus they will allow a better grasp of paint detailing, such as textures. The simplest option is a pair of 3X reading glasses, available in budget versions. Higher-quality types are available from an optometrist. Even more advanced, a set of prescription glasses can be tailored to a personal vision profile. There are also external aids such as lamps with a magnifying glass built in, and the useful headband type known as an optivisor. With this type of aid it is possible to take modelling to another level, as it becomes possible to see and work more precisely.

The following tools are also useful in a World War I modeller's toolbox:

Glue: Necessary for putting all the parts together. It can also be used to reinforce parts such as paper or tissue. Be wary of the toxic effects of many adhesives, and always take care when using cyanoacrylate, superglues and their accelerators.

Knives, scalpels, sharp and blunt blades: All of these have their uses for refining and removing unnecessary detail, as well as shaping putty.

Files: Small rat-tail files used by jewellers are perfect for cleaning up and reaming barrels.

Toothpicks: Adapt these by sanding and sharpening the ends, then seal them with superglue to harden the tips.

Tip

Store superglues in the fridge as many are temperature sensitive. Do allow them to return to room temperature before using.

Rulers: A steel ruler is important for the straight-edge cutting of straps and reins, as well as cutting parts for accessories or conversions.

Dental tools: These are useful fine tools for all manner of applications, as small flat files, sharp points, hatching for patterns and scooping out undercuts.

Jeweller awls: Helpful for punching out small buttons from lead foil. They are also invaluable for embossing circular details, especially round raised domes on webbing.

Saws, snips and scissors: Needed to trim plastic parts from sprues. Use razor saws for removing resin moulding blocks.

Spares box: A modeller's treasure chest containing spares left over from other projects, such as heads, hands and accessories parts. Sheets of veneer wood, balsa, reels of electrical and plumber's tape, coils of wire, plastic sheet, shapes and rod can also be added.

Motor tool: Can be used to speed up carving, shaping and drilling. When using with resin be aware of the dust risk: this can be suppressed by keeping the part wet, or by working with a water- or air-extraction system.

LIGHTING

Good lighting is essential for all artists, and even more so with miniature painting. This allows for better mixing and truer colours to be seen. It is also avoids having to restrict painting times to daylight, if the correct lamps are part of the modelling workbench. Cool LED or daylight bulbs are recommended to supplement natural room

A well-lit workbench with easy access to tools, paints and reference materials helps with efficient and effective modelling.

lighting and should be positioned directly over the working area. This lighting set-up can also be used for photography.

PHOTOGRAPHY

Digital photography is part of modelling today, with mobiles and cameras always on hand for capturing final photos to share finished projects. More importantly these have also become a powerful 'work in progress' tool to use for checking and adjusting flaws or incomplete parts. A couple of recommended items to help achieve high-quality images are a light booth to help channel and focus the light, plus a tripod to ensure steady, clear shots. Neither of these items need be expensive – however, it is often worth investing in a higher-specification camera if you want to print or publish your photos.

TIP

Use tech cleaning putty to remove dust from your camera, lens, lights and desk set-up to reduce contamination of figures during photographing sessions.

A basic photography set-up includes a tripod to reduce any movement of the camera and a light box to control lighting.

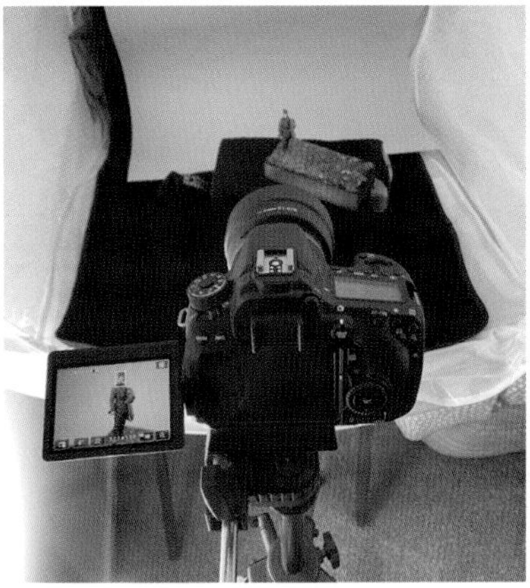

A DSLR camera, with macro lens, is useful for high-quality images. The key settings to understand are shutter speed and aperture.

Chapter Three

Basic Model Figure Construction

> **TIP**
>
> Choose a suitable personal name for your figures projects. This creates an emotional link to your art that will help deepen your understanding and interest in the chosen subject.

The most important skills to develop in miniature artistry are not only how to apply putty or paint, but also the ability to carefully develop an eye and an attention for detail. Capturing every small aspect in miniature is what makes the difference between a basic figure and one that makes a real statement. Details such as the gaps under epaulettes, lifted pocket corners, or the front edge of boots curled up, are all ways to truly represent how a person – a soldier – looks in reality: how they hold their rifle or weapon, and how they slouch, sit or lie, all depend upon their surroundings. It also expresses how they feel. It is necessary to truly understand and analyse people, considering techniques, light, shade and every detail to make a figure appear human, a living organic creature.

> **TIP**
>
> Study figures and real people closely in order to spot small details – pockets, cuffs, boots, collars – that might otherwise be missed, or which might not be practical on commercial figures. Refine and rework these details on your figures to give them a more realistic look.

PREPARING AND CONSTRUCTING RESIN FIGURE KITS

These kits feature 'John' and 'Jimmy', Privates, 29th Battalion, of the Australian Imperial Forces; at Vauvillers, 1918.

A well-known photo depicting the remains of a platoon of Diggers – the ANZAC term for infantrymen – from the 29th Battalion inspired Phil Walden to do a couple of figures from this group (the photo was shared by Barry Crook on Flickr, and contained useful reference information on the Diggers). One was John Arlow, depicted in a happy moment casually resting on his shovel, with a big smile on his face sharing a joke with a mate. This is a fine figure, which is sadly now out of production. It is worthwhile studying Phil's design and his depiction of this single figure. 'John' is centrally posed on a circular base, with one leg raised up on a battle-damaged slope. He is hunched forwards under the heavy load he carries, his right hand gripping his knees. The bulk of the figure is well balanced by the cutaway base, with the overall figure height equalling the base height.

Arlow's unit are all photographed wearing their entrenching tools over their groin, an example of applying learning from battlefield experience.

Another figure chosen from the photo is Private James 'Jimmy' Cryer. This man has been produced as a 120mm figure kit by OzMods, and is used here to explain how to clean up, assemble and prepare a typical resin figure for painting.

This kit comes in eleven pink resin parts. It is common for many resin kits to have large blocks still attached, used by the caster to pour resin into the rubber mould. These take time and care to remove, as thin parts can be very brittle and fracture easily. Fortunately this kit only has one excess pouring block on the top of the lower torso. It will be removed with a thin razor saw, then sanded smooth. The figure has basic webbing equipment and his.303 SMLE, which soldiers also call the 'Smelly' rifle.

When moving forward, soldiers were fully laden down, as is Arlow here, with their pack, greatcoat, shelter and spare Lewis gun magazine.

TIP

Before painting, carefully wash the assembled resin figures in warm soapy water with a large soft brush to remove any mould-release agent or sanding residue.

SIMPLE CONVERSION OF A RESIN FIGURE

This kit, sculpted by Phil Walden, is a 1:16 figure of an Australian Lewis Gunner of the Wellington Infantry during the Western Front campaigns of 1916–18. It has been re-released by the Australian small business OzMods. This company's figures are well cast, capturing the detail of Phil's original masters, and are highly recommended.

The figure has a nice combination of extra surface textures to simulate in paint. It has the normal serge battledress, webbing and Lewis gun, and also a rubberized groundsheet, a painted metal helmet and hessian sack leg coverings. An added challenge could be to attempt to show rain dripping off the soldier's equipment and soaking his clothing.

This conversion is intended as a tribute to the author's great-great uncle, Fred, who was killed in action on the first day of the infamous Third Battle of Ypres, also known as Passchendaele. Fred was

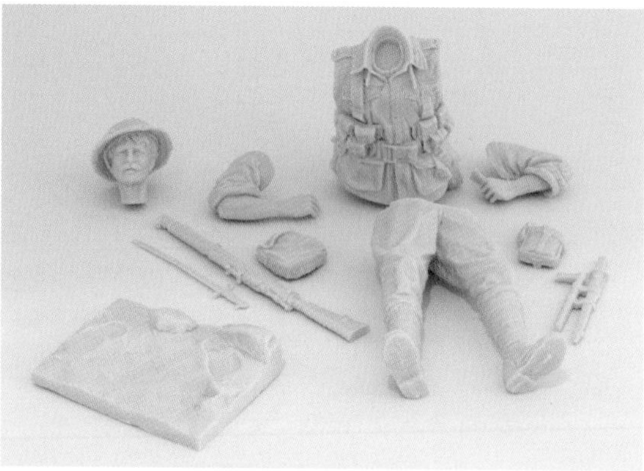

Parts layout for this kit, crisply moulded in an unusual pink that shows detail, and is a neutral colour on to which paint can be directly applied.

Always 'dry fit' and test the parts of a figure kit before gluing them together, to identify areas that need extra attention or filling.

Assembling the Figure

Important Steps	Key Points
1. Check parts	* Lay out the parts and confirm that all have been supplied. * Look for defects – mould shift along mould lines, broken parts, poor moulding, sink holes or seam lines.
2. Test fit parts	* Assemble sections or the whole figure to identify fit issues – more obvious ones are moulding blocks. * Check the sit of attached webbing components – some may need filling. * Use Blu Tack to hold parts temporarily when checking. * Look for parts or sections that could become obscured when gluing or painting other parts.
3. Remove excess resin	* Use a fine razor saw. * Keep parts wet while working to avoid dust build-up. * Give a final clean by shaving down the resin with a sharp blade.

(Continued)

Continued

Important Steps	Key Points
4. Refine the detail	* Look for any details that would benefit from repair, correction or addition. * Clean undercuts around the collar, in the cuffs, under the jacket. * Thin the straps, webbing and brackets to give a more scale effect.
5. Secure sections	* Drill holes in mating parts, particularly the neck, arms and feet. * Consider doing this also for hanging webbing items such as the bayonet frog, water bottle and entrenching tool. * Use pins or paperclips cut to size to connect parts. * Use two-part epoxy glue to lock the sections. * Small parts can be superglued. * These paperclips can be used as handles for painting and adding parts later.
6. Fill gaps	* Use either modelling putty or two-part epoxy putty to fill smaller gaps. * Pay attention to the natural fit of webbing equipment.
7. Add final details	* Try to assemble as much of the figure as possible prior to painting. This avoids having to glue parts on to painted surfaces. * Be wary of adding parts that may obscure areas and make it difficult to paint them. If necessary these can be underpinned with matt black or another dark base colour. * Avoid adding fragile parts such as bayonets that can easily be knocked or snapped off during painting.

Tip

When using a grinder or when sanding resin, always wear a dust mask, or if possible keep working surfaces wet in order to minimize resin dust.

an infantryman in the Wellington Regiment, engaged in a night-time assault on the township of La Basseville. The weather was bad over the period leading up to this battle. The plan is to show Fred moving up into the line before the battle, trudging through the mud of recent rains.

In order to make this simple conversion more distinctively 'EnZed', Fred wears the iconic peaked felt hat known as the 'lemon squeezer'. This became associated with the New Zealand troops in World War I. It has a peaked crown with four dents and a flat brim. Like the Australian slouch hat, it was often worn whenever practical, rather than the heavier steel helmet.

Phil's AIF ANZAC – Jimmy Cryer, produced by OzMods – favours a darker, more sombre palette painted with a blend of oils and enamels.

Original master figure for a Lewis gunner, with some pre-painted parts, separated ready for casting in resin by OzMods.

After cleaning up the resin using a sharp knife, the original is reworked with white Apoxie brand epoxy putty. The main adjustments are described in the table.

ENZED DEFINED

EnZed stands for NZ, from 'Johnny EnZed', the more common name used by New Zealanders to identify themselves, in the same way as 'Tommy' is used for British soldiers. 'Kiwi' was not widely adopted until post-World War I.

Fred conversion version 1 began with an Apoxie putty lemon squeezer. Unfortunately it did not look correct as the peaked crown was too broad and too short.

Version 2 added soft putty and green Blu Tack, to test a taller height and new shape for the hat.

Small sections of tissue paper soaked with superglue were used for ragged edging added to the old sandbag leg wraps.

The finished kit by Mark Dunsmuir: the face in oils, the uniform a mixture of oils and enamels, with matt varnish for the final coat; the remainder consisted of enamels.

Assembling the Figure

Important Steps	Key Points
1. Rework the face	* Carefully carve off the moustache to give a clean-shaven face as Fred appeared in pre-deployment and Egypt photos.
2. Rework the upper body	* Hollow out the edges of the groundsheet at the back and inside edges. * Add a larger scarf, so it slips down over the groundsheet, plus an altered pipe. * Reverse the gas-mask haversack flap.
3. Rework the lower torso	* The lower front panels of the jacket indicate an Australian jacket, with separate balloon pockets and front panel seams. * Use epoxy putty to fill the seams and bulk out the pockets, smoothing the sides into the jacket. * Replace the Australian buttoned cuffs with the standard open cuff on the British-issued jacket. * Hollow out the helmet with the motor tool and reposition it over the top of the satchel; use a little putty to add a small section of visible helmet strap.
4. Build the hat	* It did take time to get the Lemon Squeezer looking right. * These hats varied a lot, quickly losing their uniform shape due to the effect of weather conditions on the soft felt. * The brim is epoxy putty rolled out flat, then positioned on the head; its floppy edges are pushed in with a rubber brush as the putty cures. * The peaked crown begins as a blob of putty, then build it up and shape it using rubber brushes. * Further refinement is done once it is in place on the brim; this crown took three attempts before it was finished.
5. Detail the leg wraps	* Ragged edging is added from tissue.

Making Changes: Epoxy Putty Modifications

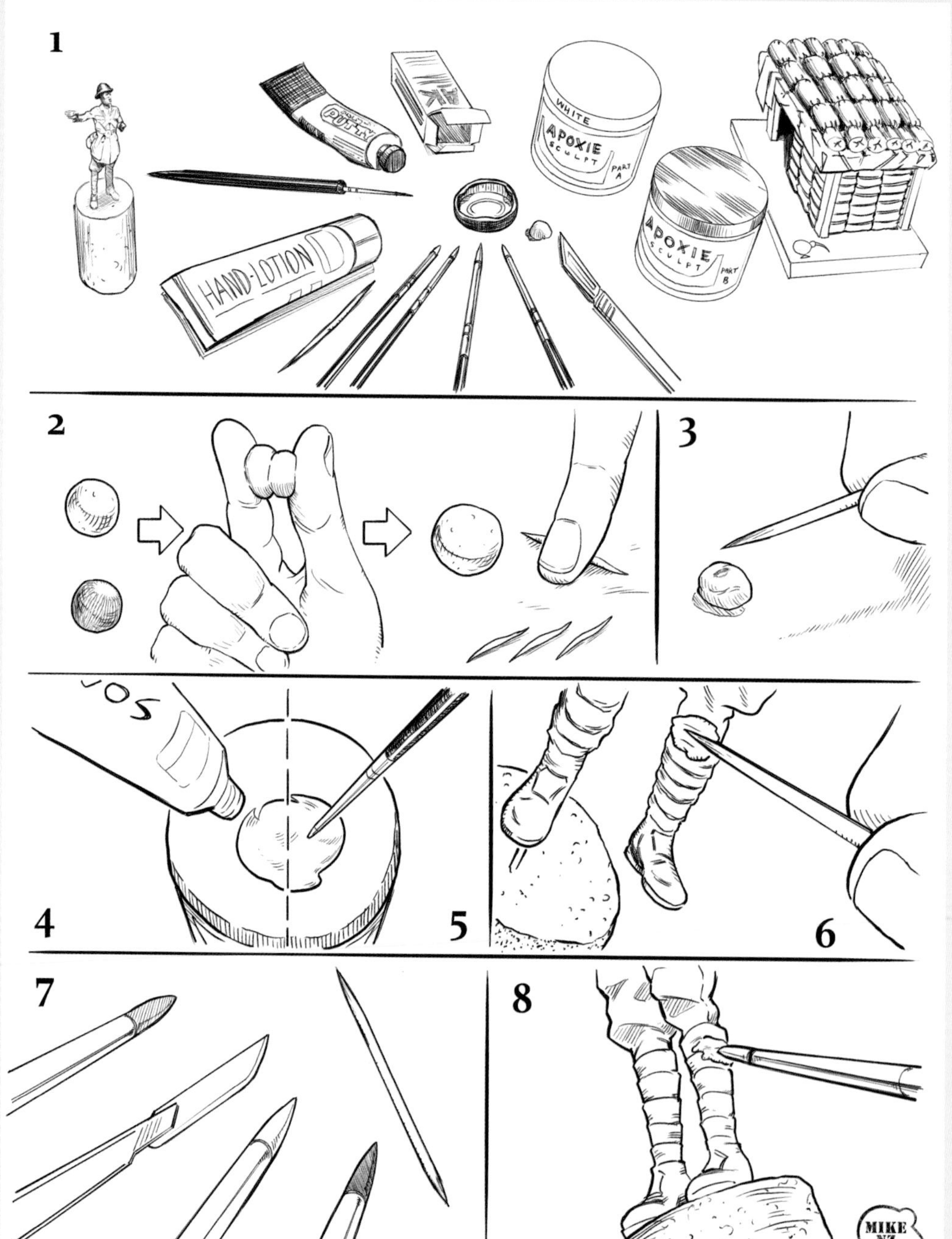

(Continued)

Continued

Tip: Apply barrier hand cream to the hands to protect against putty grease, and when filling gaps or sculpting use hand cream to smooth the putty.

1. Materials for filling and forming shapes (from 12 o'clock):
   * AK acrylic putty – tube and box
   * Apoxie two-part air-drying putty
   * Large blunt-bladed scalpel
   * Rubber shaping brushes
   * Hand lotion
   * Sharpened toothpick
   * Old paintbrush
2. Blend the putty:
   * Create two small similar-sized balls from Part A and Part B.
   * Squeeze the balls together and knead between the fingers.
   * Ensure they are thoroughly mixed to a single uniform colour.
   * Roll out thin threads of putty in the palm of your hand with a finger.
3. Use a sharpened toothpick to select a small blob to fill and reshape the gap.
4. Squeeze a small amount of hand lotion on to a dark surface, such as Part B black lid.
5. Moisten the rubber brush with hand lotion to help smooth and work the putty surface.
6. Use a toothpick to add putty to the area to be filled or for building extra detail. Push the putty into position with the toothpick.
7. Use different rubber shaper brushes and blunt scalpel blades to push and move the softened putty around.
8. Fill the gap and make a new detail:
   * A rubber brush ensures the gap is filled and can be used to add softer detail.
   * Use a sharp pointed toothpick or blades to create and make sharp detail.
   * Smooth the putty surface with hand lotion on a paintbrush and shapers.

Tip: It is easier to work with small balls of putty, rather than large blobs, as this helps to ensure that the putty is thoroughly mixed and will cure fully.

Chapter Four

Paints and Painting Equipment

OIL PAINTS

Oil paints are based on a coloured pigment suspended in an oil base. This means they take time to dry, depending on both the pigment and the oil mix. They also have a tendency to dry with a gloss finish, an undesirable sheen when used for cotton or matt clothing.

The longer drying time does make them easier to blend, and the sheen is particularly helpful when painting flesh, leather surfaces, and horse and animal fur. Drying time can be accelerated with the application of gentle heat from a light bulb, ideally in an enclosed space – for example, a small wooden box lined with aluminium foil to reflect and contain heat. This can also help matt colours.

Oils are versatile, their vibrant colours retaining all their brightness when fully dried, and can be easily mixed with each other to get any desired colour. An appreciation of the colour wheel is useful as oils are sold in primary and secondary colours, which do need to be mixed to attain colour matches with World War I uniforms and equipment.

Oils are supplied in tubes. Because of their rich colour a tiny bit goes far, and if stored well, paint should last for many years. Note that if the tube caps are not cleaned before closing they can become impossible to remove. Soaking the tube tops in boiling water for five minutes or so allows the paint residue to soften, making caps easier to remove.

Oils are easily thinned with white spirit or turpentine. Odourless thinners make these more user-friendly, especially when cleaning surfaces and brushes, however these may not be as effective when mixing paint, or blending on a figure, and may make washes dry glossy. Therefore it is advisable to test a thinner on a spare figure or hidden surface to make sure it works as expected. Warm water and soap is often a useful follow-up to thinners with oil-paint-laden brushes.

Well-thinned paints are useful for adding washes and transparent glazes for soft or deep shadowing. Thinned paint will more reliably dry matt, although this does depend upon the thinner used. Various mediums can also be used to ensure a consistent gloss, sheen or matt finish. Again, test these in terms of drying time and desired effect before using on a figure or bust. The long working time of oils thinned and unthinned with intense colours, and good coverage with even the smallest amount of paint, is very useful for shading metal

Tip

If a matt effect is required when using oil paints, squeezing paint on to a paper palette and leaving it for ten to twenty minutes will draw oil out of the paint and speed up the drying time.

TIP

Oils can be messy to work with, and some colours, cleaning agents and mediums are toxic. Always keep brushes away from the mouth when using.

Oil paints typically come in foil tubes, which if handled and stored properly, will keep paint usable for decades.

surfaces – for example, adding a 'blued' effect or oily residue, as well as for weapon woodwork that requires a soft polished and oiled sheen.

The main oil brands referred to in this book are Archival, Rembrandt, Rowney, and Winsor and Newton (W&N).

ACRYLIC PAINTS

Modern polymer acrylic paints have revolutionized miniature figure art with their water-based composition, making them safer and more user-friendly than the earlier oil, enamel and lacquer hobby paints. They are still evolving and are regularly being upgraded with purportedly more reliability in finish, mixing capacity and lustre. They are easily mixed with a good shake, or with a wooden toothpick or matchstick. Some modellers add small ball bearings to the plastic bottles to ensure they can mix the sediment with the thinner, which quickly separates out if left standing.

There is a bewildering range of pre-mixed colours from almost all paint makers, who all claim that their selection is the only one a modeller requires. In reality, while some colours are particularly useful to have 'off the shelf' – for example World War I uniform tones – it is often more important to determine the effect or finish you are trying to achieve. Acrylic ranges all have different properties, making some more suited for surfaces requiring sheen, and others that need a matt texture to be built up. Experiment widely with those paints most readily available, and only seek out others if the desired results or colours are not being achieved for what is needed for a project.

Another main advantage of acrylics is the quick drying time, which allows overpainting, and also allows surroundings to be painted in the same session without fear of unwanted mixing. Thin layers can be built up and merged together with various slightly different colour tones. This quick drying can be a challenge if you are used to slower-drying oils or enamels. A wet palette is a helpful aid in prolonging the working time and life of acrylics.

One frustration that can arise with acrylics is clouding of the paint, which appears as a chalkiness as the paint dries. This often occurs when poor-quality water is used for mixing, and minerals settle out of the dry paint; it can often be resolved by using bottled, purified or boiled water. If it persists try another paint brand.

Other annoyances with acrylics can be their very transparent colour, and their low adherence to smooth surfaces. Using an enamel primer can help avoid this; alternatively, build up a couple of extra thin layers rather than being tempted to add a thicker layer.

The following are the main acrylic brands, with the abbreviations used in this book in brackets:

* AK Interactive (AK)
* Citadel (C)
* Golden Fluid Acrylics
* Jo Sonja (JS)
* LifeColor (LC)
* Master Series Paint (MSP)
* Matisse
* P3
* ScaleColour (SC)
* Vallejo (V), plus a sub-brand Game Colour (GC)

GOUACHE

Gouache is a form of non-toxic watercolour paint that uses natural pigment and is interchangeable with acrylics. It has a more opaque and reliably smooth matt finish. It comes in large plastic tubes. The main brand is Jo Sonja (JS), which has played an important role in lifting the overall standard of painting because of its ease of use. Originally introduced to miniaturists by South Korean artists, these paints have become more readily available and are now a part of many figure painters' resources.

Acrylics come in all sizes and shapes, in tubes, bottles, jars and boxed sets. Most are mixable between brands.

The drying time for gouache is similar to acrylics, and this can be extended using water colour blending mediums: these are a denser, clearer, water-like liquid that help to blend colours. Try Windsor and Newton's 'Water Colour Blending Medium' or Vallejo's 'Glazing Medium'. Both are suitable for gouache, acrylics and other water-based paints.

ENAMELS

Humbrol enamels were specifically developed for model makers and hobbyists in the latter half of the twentieth century, supplied in small tins. If the tin lids are well secured and airtight the paints will last for many years. Japanese suppliers, such as Tamiya, chose a larger glass jar, which is easier to open and close.

Enamel paints are designed to have a gloss, satin or matt finish; they require thorough mixing to ensure that the desired sheen level is maintained. The most useful way to mix them properly is by shaking them, or by using a stainless-steel rod or similar. It is important to ensure the sediment is well mixed. An alternative method is to take a drop of paint, using a solid plastic rod or wooden stirrer, then to mix this directly on a non-absorbent surface such as a kitchen tile or painter's plastic palette. Make sure the palette can contain the paint, as enamels flow quickly when thinned.

Drying time is reasonably quick but allows enough time for smooth blending, when thinner is used to feather the edges of colours. Enamels are more reliable for washes, and when used with recommended thinner will normally dry as matt or satin.

Enamel thinning agents – turpentine or mineral spirits – are toxic, so in the same way as with oils, care should be taken when using them. Make sure to have well-ventilated work spaces to avoid any build-up of fumes.

Enamels can be supplied in aerosol cans, and as such are useful primers, especially for groundwork and metal figures. Again, make sure any spray

Enamels and lacquers, often supplied in cans or glass jars due to their solvent base, produce amazing metallic effects due to actual metal pigments.

painting is done in a wide open area or within a spray booth so that over-spray and paint mist is captured.

Because of their strong, protective and dense covering properties, enamels are ideal for groundwork. They bond well with most surfaces, especially smooth surfaces, hence their value as a primer, but they will also cover rough, uneven surfaces such as earth, plaster and vegetation.

LACQUER PAINTS

Lacquer paint is more commonly used for larger applications such as painting cars, but has been bottled in hobby-sized containers by companies such as Gunze Sangyo. The Mr Colour range of metallics is particularly useful for large-scale World War I figure and bust painting. These paints allow for the most realistic effects, unequalled with other paints, as actual metallic pigment is flowed smoothly on to the desired area. Once dry this is polished with cotton buds, or soft polishing wheels in a motor tool. Nothing beats their effect when they are worked up with polishing and oil-paint weathering.

The downside with lacquers is their toxic and volatile formulation. Denatured alcohol is also used as a thinner. As it quickly evaporates it is important to have painting brushes and tools ready at hand to flow the colour quickly on to the figure's surface. A good aspect is that micro-thin layers of these lacquers can be built up over each other, with each becoming harder the longer they are left before polishing.

PRINTER'S INKS, POWDERS, PIGMENTS AND PASTELS

Another painting medium that can provide pleasing metal effects are the inks and powders used by printers or make-up artists. These come either already mixed as a thick paste, suspended in an oily binding mix, or in powder form. They can be mixed with mediums such as enamel varnish, or Windsor and Newton's liquin. These additives are necessary to help drying time and to improve the appearance of the final colours. The thicker composition also helps make the inks more controllable when painting fine detail such as badges.

The results with inks are very effective, with a soft, muted metallic effect and a genuine lustre suitable for weapons, mess tins, metal buttons and suchlike.

An advantage of inks is that they mix easily with oil paints. This allows for subtle variation in tones, such as shading and highlighting weapons and metal equipment parts.

Printer's inks require the same safe handling as oils, enamels and lacquers, though their thickness makes them easier to control, meaning they make less mess.

Other powder colouring materials are pigments and pastels used for weathering and groundwork effects. These are added with a thin wash, or using brushes or sponges in a dusting fashion. They remain loose materials, so can be smudged off if handling figures after use. Depending on the type of pigment, they can sometimes be sealed with a light spray of matt varnish. Brands include Faber Castell, AK Interactive, Vallejo, Secret Weapon, Ammo by Mig Jimenez, Tamiya, and Humbrol.

THINNERS AND MEDIUMS

An area needing constant practice and experimentation when painting miniatures is the use of thinners and mediums. A rule to this is 'You can always add more, but you can't take any away', so the key is to add sparingly. Learning how to better understand the way thinners and mediums work with paint will pay dividends in controlling paint effects such as texturing.

Thinners are best prepared ready for use in small containers. Small portions can be easily dipped into with a brush, or using a pipette dropper to dispense small amounts on to the paint palette.

Before applying freshly thinned paint to the figure, check the paint consistency. With water-based acrylics, do this by dabbing on to the hand; with toxic paints, use an edge of the palette or a tissue.

Mediums are solutions that cause the paint to react in a particular way, including flattening, blending, crackling, glossing and glazing. Each of these mediums can be used on their own, or in combination with others to create different effects with the paint. Some examples of this mixing will be shown in the projects presented in this book.

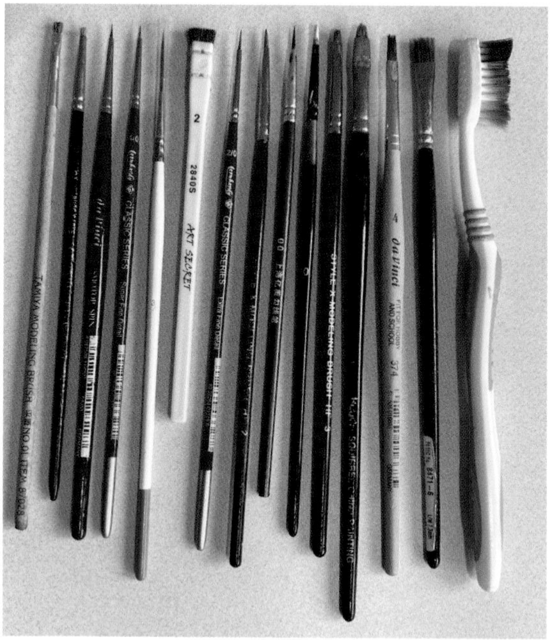

Paintbrushes come in a variety of shapes, sizes and quality. This selection is most commonly used for projects in this book.

PAINTBRUSHES

So much has been written about the right brushes to use that it can seem as if these are the silver bullet to painting greatness. Certainly brushes are important tools, but they don't need to be expensive to be useful. Almost any artist or hobby brush can have an appropriate use for the miniature painter. It is familiarity with how to use the brushes that is more important than the brushes themselves. Brush brands include Style X, Vallejo, da Vinci, Windsor and Newton, Pebeo, Citadel, Rosemary & Co, and Broken Toad.

Natural Bristles

Brushes generally come with either natural or artificial bristles. Natural fur includes sable, squirrel, fitch, badger, and pig or hog. For miniatures the softer sables are often chosen as they hold paint, and a point, well. They are a more expensive natural brush, so cheaper squirrel may be better value for those on a budget, or where a point is less important, such as with a shaped brush. Coarser pig or hog are suitable for groundwork and some weathering techniques, where precise brushstrokes are less necessary, and instead random paint splatters offer a more effective finish. Washing brushes regularly in warm soapy water or with a brush-cleaner medium will extend the life of the bristles.

For World War I miniatures it is recommended that where practical, a set of sables, either red or Kolinsky, are added to your painting kit. They can be used for flesh and fine detail painting.

Synthetic Bristles

Synthetic brushes are more affordable and can imitate natural fur, with bristles made from nylon or polyester blends. A feature of these is that they can be more robust and more forgiving, and do not require as much attention to cleaning. However, they do have a limited usable lifespan, especially when shape or point is important. Synthetics are adequate for general-purpose painting and texturing because this can take a toll on brush tips.

Brushes come in a variety of shapes. Those more suitable for painting miniatures are pointed and flats, while short stippling brushes can be made from old, worn ones that have become unsuitable for their original use. A few special-purpose brushes are useful, such as a couple of longer pointed riggers for fine lines, as seen on corduroy trousers, and wedged flat brushes to recreate the ribbing on webbing.

Air Brushes

Some modellers use these tools to prime and lay in preliminary shading, or lighting on figures. Bigger figures and busts can also have main areas quickly painted with an airbrush. Special lighting and weathering effects can be achieved by the soft, gentle spraying. However, it is still necessary to finish the figures using regular brushes where paint control is more precise.

Making a Wet Palette

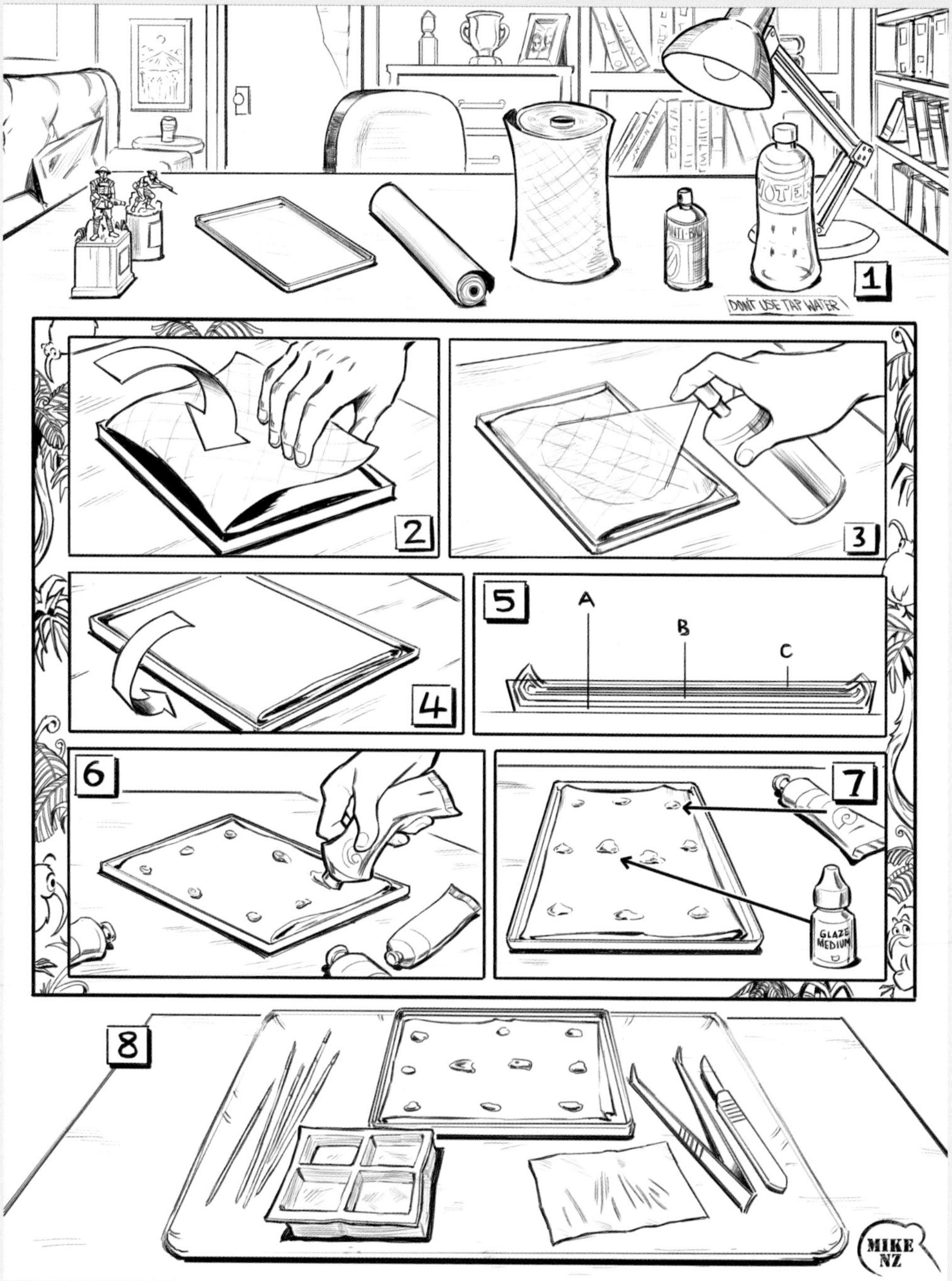

(Continued)

Continued

What is a wet palette and why should I use one? One of the biggest challenges that painters find when using acrylics is their quick drying time. Although it is possible to add a retarder to the paint to slow drying, this can affect how the paint flows or the sheen when it is dry. Instead, many artists use a wet palette – like a mini humidifier – to keep acrylics moist while they are being used. Paint can last for weeks using this simple tool, and can be revitalized if the paint starts to dry. This is particularly helpful when using the same mixes over more than one painting session.

Tip: Use only enough water to keep the paper towel wet: too much and it will flood the paint. You can always add more water if the towel starts to dry. If too much water is added simply leave the lid off for a while to allow excess moisture to evaporate; to rehydrate the paint and paper, sit the lid back over the tray.

How to Make a Wet Palette

1. Ingredients for a wet palette (L–R): takeaway tray, baking paper, paper towel, antibacterial spray, filtered or bottled water.
2. Fold the paper towel into the base of the tray.
3. Spray light anti-bacterial spray on to the paper towel.
4. Fold the baking paper over and under the edges of the paper towel. This prevents the paper curling up when it is moistened.
5. Add water to the tray (A), just enough to wet the paper towel (B) but not swamping the baking paper (C).
6. Add drops of acrylic paint from tubes or bottles around the edges of the palette.
7. In the centre of the tray drop glaze medium at one end, and as required, varnish drops at the other end.
8. The final layout ready for painting (L–R): brushes, water tray for brush washing, wet palette, tissue to remove surplus water or test paint flow, tweezers, and scalpel for removing lint.

Tip: An alternative way of testing paint flow before applying it to a figure is to brush it on to your thumbnail or the fleshy part of your thumb.

Chapter Five

Painting Figures

PAINTING TECHNIQUES

My four main painting techniques are stibbling, stippling, dabbing and stabbing. I first developed these to paint busts, and then later adapted them to paint figures. Stippling and dabbing will be familiar to many who paint with oils and acrylics; stibbling and stabbing combine these well-known techniques with a purposeful effort to carefully build a slight texture into the paint surface.

Painting is an individual and personal endeavour, so please use these notes and thoughts to create your own style with your own projects.

Stippling: This technique applies small dots of the same colour to build up lighter and darker tones. This is done by jabbing the figure surface with a pointed brush tip or a round brush with a cropped top. It results in a smooth, regular coloured surface of similar tone with rough dotting of different colour hues.

Dabbing: This technique applies irregular splotches, and blends paint by roughly overlapping edges of colour. The result is a smoother surface, and when satin varnish and glazing medium are included they help to achieve a translucent skin effect.

Stibbling: This is a paint texturing effect where the brush sides and edges do the paintwork. These are used in a gentle stabbing motion to progressively build layers of paint. This results in linear spots, splotches and scratches of various colours that simulate rough surfaces and materials. This also helps blend areas together in an irregular and natural way, whilst creating a visible texture. A face is an ideal surface to see all three effects (*see* the example and detail in 'Vic' in Chapter 7), whereas the bulk of the uniform and webbing mainly uses stippling or stibbling for heavier texture or weathering.

Stabbing: This technique uses drier paint, which leaves tiny spots and rough surface texture.

Note: Remember detail is still aiming to be in scale to the naked eye, so can only be appreciated though magnification and photos.

Each technique is difficult to explain in words, so an illustrated plate shared here tries to show and explain these further. Do also study the large photos of the finished projects, as these will give more insights and a sense of what each finished effect looks like when applied.

TIP

Suggest detail with textures: the viewer's eye will complete the illusion by filling the gaps and imagining what the real fabric or material looks like.

Painting Tips, Techniques and Brushstrokes

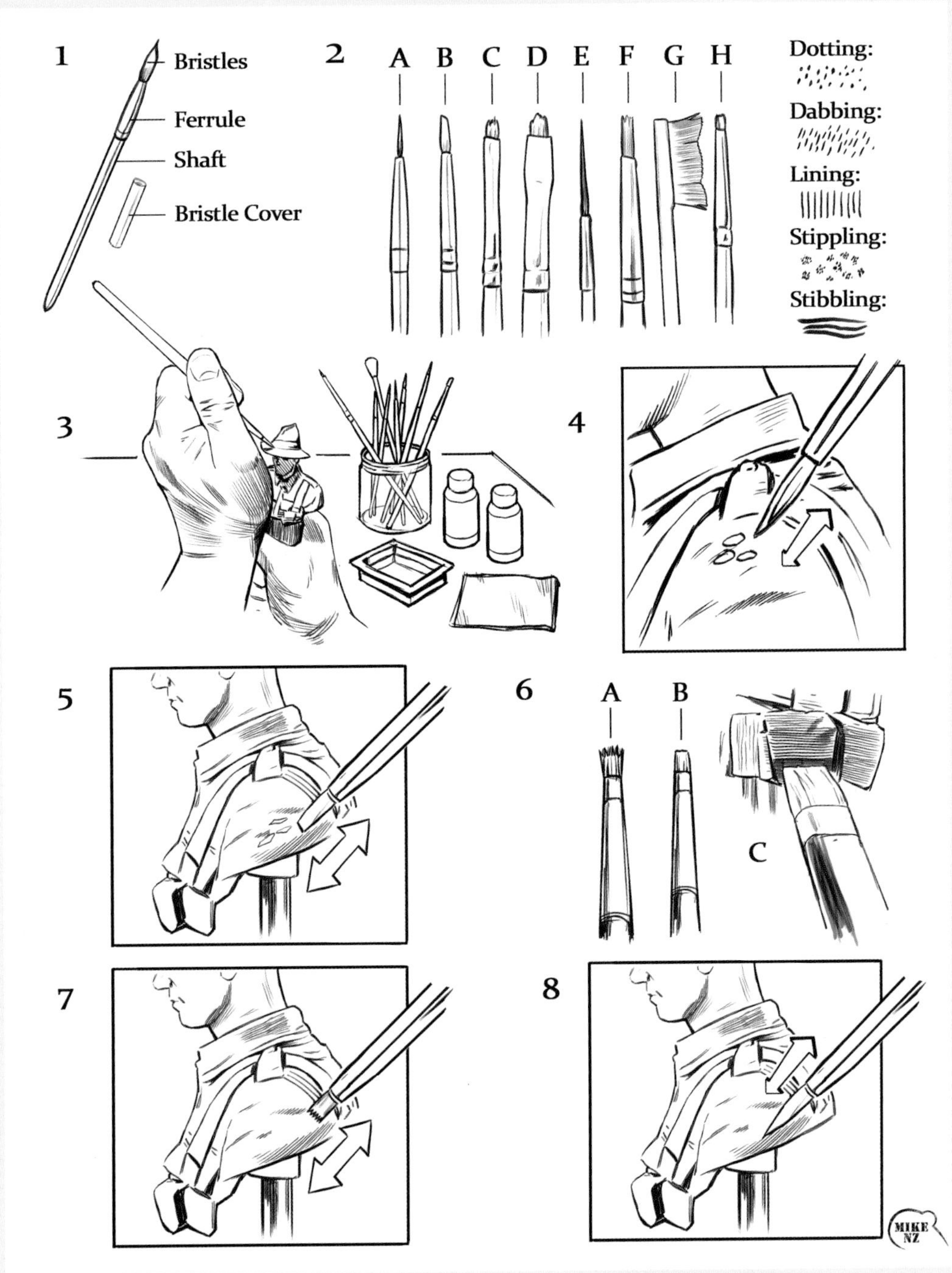

(Continued)

Continued

1. Know your tools:
Bristle cover: A small clear tube, essential for protecting points; it can be cut from tubing if a cover is not supplied or is lost.
Bristles: Protect these with regular cleaning. When they fray, use for other texturing effects – for example, crop off the paintbrush top and use it for stippling. (2H.)
Ferrule: Make sure it is tight; if not, secure it with glue.
Shaft: This should be a maximum of two hand-widths long. Some brands come with a longer artist shaft, in which case remove the excess length.

2. Types of brush and the paint effects from each:
(*See also* the brushes photo in Chapter 4, Paints and Painting Equipment.)
A, B: Pointed sables, sizes 10/0–2
C, D: Flat sable or squirrel, sizes 1–3
E: Sable liner 3/0
F: Flat synthetic 4 da Vinci
G: Old soft toothbrush
H: Crop top: originally a pointed sable with half bristles cut off, sizes 1–2

Brush Types Suitable for Different Techniques

Technique	Brush Type	Purpose	Effect
Dotting	A, B	Precise detail for clothing, wear and flesh texture detail such as fine wool and skin spots	Individual, irregular-sized spots
Dabbing	B, C, D, F	Softer textures for fine material clothing such as cotton or silk, also flesh and leather toning	Irregular splotches and broader dashes
Lining	A, E	Preliminary shadowing before texture, and deep shadow or highest highlights	Narrow lines around seams, pockets and edging
Stippling	B, C, D, F, H	Coarse material: serge, wool and lighter weathering; dust. With a flat brush: webbing ribbing	Groups of irregular broken spots and stripes
Stabbing	C, D, F	Rough clothing and heavy weathering – mud	Rough, heavy splotches
Stibbling	B, C, D	Blend and integrate textures	Frayed, irregular broken strokes
Drybrushing	C, D, F	Highlighted surface detail, especially on equipment and weapons. Can be too harsh for large-scale figure clothing	Irregular strokes of semi-dry paint remnants on raised surfaces

(Continued)

Continued

Technique	Brush Type	Purpose	Effect
Oiling leather	G	Allows a lighter base to appear through a dark oil-paint overcoat	Increased transparency on central and upper area
Pastels or pigments	D, H	Ingrained dirt and weathering	Rub or scrub dry pastel/ pigment into surface

3. Holding and Painting a Bust:
* Other painting items are laid out tidy and ready for action in the background.
* Keep a strong grip on the holder. Stretch out the arm from time to time to check the overall appearance of painting effects and tones.
* Lock the elbows into the side of the body when painting fine detail.
* Relax the arms when painting texture to allow more movement of the brush tip.

4. Dotting: A quick in/out brush action, moving from larger to smaller dots.
5. Dabbing: Move the brush back and forth, letting the thinned paint flow broadly into other areas.
6. Stippling: The effect will depend on the brush bristles – splayed (A) for fabric, or tighter and flat (B) for more precise texture such as on webbing ribs.
7. Stabbing: The brush is pushed firmly into and along the surface. Note this is hard on brushes, so use old or cheap brushes.
8. Stibbling: Use the side of the brush, moving it in and out, and pushing it on to the surface so the bristles splay out, leaving an erratic pattern. This is particularly useful for final highlighting, and for blending and softening other textures together.

Tip: Not all brushes are soft – tease out oils and thick acrylics with a toothpick or darning needle to simulate fur and hair.

PAINTING BELGIANS

The table and photos below depict the Belgian infantryman's uniform as it changed from the start of war to late in the war. I am indebted to Henk Devos for his support on this topic, and to David Moortgat, the supplier and model in the photos.

Painting an Armoured Car Crew

Copper State Models (CSM) has begun developing an expanding series of 1:35 World War I armoured car models for a long-neglected market. Included so far are Allied machines from Belgium, the UK, Canada, Italy and Russia. As their popularity grows, more have been planned, including vehicles from France and the USA. This in turn has opened up a desire for figures to accompany these more esoteric models. The production of personnel to man these kits has been started by Copper State themselves, as well as Yellow House Club and ModelCellar, the figures sculpted by the always reliable Mike Good.

Among CSM releases is this group of five 1:35 Belgians: Léon, Henri, Pierre, Étienne and Thierry; they date from 1915–17. Three are from the more colourful uniformed 'Intermediate' period – Pierre, Étienne and Thierry – and the other two – Léon and Henri – are from the later 'Green' period (*see* below). These latter two can represent either crewmen or infantry in support of the armoured cars, one option being as members of the small motorized force known as the Belgian Armoured

Uniform Colours: Belgian Uniforms Early to Late War (1914 to 1916)

View	Key Points
1. Early uniform – front left angle	* Pre-war 'Yser' uniform, named after the river along the banks of which most of the army were based. * Pillbox cap, known as 'Camembert', with red stripe and piping. * On the front of the headgear was a national colour badge with the unit number (2nd Line Infantry), or the first letter of the fortress name: A for Antwerp, L for Liège, N for Namur. * 'Gross Bleu' coloured greatcoat had brass buttons; each one also has a '2' to denote the unit's regimental number. * On the left hip is a Linnemann pattern entrenching tool and empty bayonet scabbard. * Grey-blue trousers with thin piping down the outside leg seam (black = infantry, red = Grenadiers) * Black lace-up leather gaiters over black boots.
2. Early uniform – back	* Similar design equipment to the German infantry, with a grey blanket wrapped around cowhide pack, secured with black leather straps. * Black-painted mess tin and khaki-felted water bottle sits over brown 'bread bag'. * Greatcoat back panels were buttoned centrally.
3. Early uniform – front	* The bottom flaps of the greatcoat are folded and buttoned up to make it easier to march. * Black leather equipment harness and large ammunition pouch. * Rifle is a 7.65 Belgian Mauser Model 1889, attached with the original short bayonet with quillon.
4. Late uniform – front right angle	* Soon after their first taste of combat Belgian troops needed to change their uniform, due to scarcity of materials and battle practicality. They sourced a mix of clothing from any and all the Allies. Primarily designed, like the greatcoat here, in French style with British khaki serge. * Buttons were simplified, with the national lion symbol embossed on them and painted khaki. * Epaulettes are piped in royal blue for infantry and Grenadiers. * Corporal rank is shown by the khaki braid worn round the cuffs, with two small diagonal red 'front' stripes denoting eighteen months of frontline service – the first after one year, then one for every six months after that. * Brown boots and gaiters – a shortage of boots meant these could be made by French, British or even US suppliers.
5. Late uniform – back	* French Adrian helmet, with the lion-head badge for all arms, was adopted and covered here with a cloth cover due to the high sheen of the paint. * Large British-pattern canvas pack, with khaki lacquered mess tin. * Equipment harness varied across units, becoming brown leather or canvas webbing, dependent again upon supply. For example small ammunition pouches came from as far afield as Argentina, and British-made Mills equipment was also common. * Two waterbottles with different covering types. * Late war gas-mask holder for a Belgian M18 mask, which was adapted from the French ARS mask.
6. Late uniform – front	* French M2 gas mask, also worn by British troops in 1916, is worn as a handy reserve. Its oval canister, covered in khaki cloth, hangs from a string on the soldier's left hip. * Almost the only item that has stayed the same from early war was the Belgian Mauser, potentially now manufactured in the UK. However, now it has the long 1916 sword bayonet.

1. Early uniform – front left angle.

2. Early uniform – back.

3. Early uniform – front.

4. Late uniform – front right angle.

5. *Late uniform – back.*

6. *Late uniform – front.*

There are few other Belgians available; however, ModelCellar have a large bust and also armoured-car crewmen, including Russians, which can be adapted.

Division, which was seconded to the Russian Army in 1915. These troops operated on the Eastern Front, initially in the Belgian-built Minervas, and then later with British-supplied Lanchester armoured cars. On the fall of the Czarist regime they avoided taking sides in the civil war – instead the division shipped out of Vladivostok direct to the USA where they paraded in their regular Belgian uniforms to support recruiting efforts.

ModelCellar offer another pair of Belgians suited for this Eastern Front unit. Crews on this front wore an interesting mix of clothing, incorporating Russian items with their Belgian uniforms, such as the short leather jacket worn by Russian crew. ModelCellar also have another four Russian figures, some of which could have their heads swapped or be converted into Belgians.

I once made a rule that I would only work on one figure at a time, to ensure I did not get distracted and leave a trail of unfinished figures. However, it proved more efficient to prepare and paint this armoured-car crew all together.

Having decided to paint the five figures at one time it was necessary to first prepare and research them. All are nice little figures with subtle sculpting from Andrei Bleskin. He is an 'old school' craftsman, putting a lot of effort into drapery, especially engineering the parts

A portrait of World War I: Belgian Lancers in their traditional mounted role, and with modern technology in a little Minerva armoured car. HENK DEVOS

and undercuts below jackets and around collars. All the jackets on this group are open with no solid blocks to carve out. This feature always makes for easier painting and a more natural-looking fit of clothing. It's always better to have this, rather than painting a less-than-convincing solid black area. Casting quality is crisp, with only fine seams to be removed. They are well-thought-out designs, and assembly is straightforward.

The Belgians played an important part in World War I from the start, with the invasion of Belgium being a central justification for the Allies engaging in battle against the Central Powers. The Belgian armies were small in comparison with their French and British allies, but were known for their pluck, and their dashing uniforms: the cavalry wore brightly coloured, short braided jackets and bearskin busby hats, the carabiniers had short green jackets with yellow facings, and the infantry were dressed in long, dark blue coats with stylish shakos.

This early 1914 uniform was known as the 'Blue' period, but items deemed impractical were soon replaced by clothing better suited to modern warfare. For example, in the following 'Intermediate' period the uniforms of the Lancers were tidied up, with a little less lace and a more practical kepi. When the small Minerva armoured car arrived on the scene, the use of horses was abandoned – however, the Lancers continued to wear the same short crop jacket and long trimmed trousers, with leather reinforcement for riding at the cuff. This is how the first three CSM figures – Pierre, Étienne and Thierry – are dressed.

Identifying the Different Lancer Regiments

Lancer Regiment	Tunic Piping	Trouser Piping	Trouser Stripes x 2
1st, 2nd	Crimson red	Crimson red	White
3rd, 5th	White	White	Yellow
4th	Sky blue	Sky blue	Yellow

The 'Intermediate' Lancers: Pierre, Étienne and Thierry

These Lancers will be very similar, and part of the challenge is to bring some variety in subtle ways to each of them. Starting with their faces, all are given small variations in tone, making maximum use of a more complex flesh palette trial using mixes adapted from talented Chinese and South Korean artists, who tend to have a more vibrant palette for flesh colours. Reference photos were useful to provide colour tones for uniforms, especially trousers, and the intention here was to use basic primary colours instead of pre-mixes.

The first units operating the Minerva were the Lancer regiments, each identified by the colour of the striped trim on their tunics and outer trouser legs (*see* table).

Note: In 1917 when they moved into 'Green' period uniforms, each regiment was identified by the number centrally placed on the epaulette, plus their coloured collar tab: yellow for the 1st, 2nd and 3rd Lancers, and white for the 4th Lancers.

The 'Green' Belgians: Henri and Léon

By mid to late war the Belgian uniforms had changed completely, due to supply shortages as well as the conditions in which soldiers were serving. Henri and Léon are wearing the uniform of this 'Green' period. This khaki green is more like the colour of the uniforms worn by the British and Russians they served with, though there is still scope for a splash of colour in the collar taps and epaulette trim – red denoting infantry. Covered French Adrian-styled helmets are also supplied with the figures to further reinforce the late war appearance.

Figures are washed with detergent before painting, then the eyes are positioned (left) *and detailed, with the deepest shadow under the brow* (right).

Although Henri and Léon have simple uniforms, these do lend themselves to converting into the Belgian Division in Russia. On the Eastern Front the Armoured Car Division belonged to the artillery, whose uniform had dark blue collar patches edged in red. Shoulder straps for the ordinary gunners were plain or piped in red. Officers wore the equivalent of Russian rank shoulder boards known as 'pogoni' on their epaulettes. During the course of the campaign uniforms became a motley mix of Belgian and Russian uniform items, and anything else available that would keep the wearer warm. Leather coats were popular, and even Russian overcoats and occasionally Russian lamb-wool headgear. Mixing parts of CSM's British RNAS and the Russian Imperial Autocar Machine Gun Platoon provided really interesting figures to man Belgian armoured cars.

TIP

Use electrical insulation tape to create straps and thin reins with tension. Before use, remove the sticky side with turps, then cut with a sharp blade and a steel ruler. Stick one end in position with superglue, then when dry use tweezers to pull it taut and glue the other end into position.

Painting the Figures

Important Steps	Key Points (All paints Jo Sonja unless otherwise stated)
1. Paint eyes – all	Sequence devised for this group: *Base*: Vallejo Light Flesh *Iris*: Carbon Black, with focus on position, shape and size of this *Detail*: Upper lash in Black, thinned Napthol Red Light in corners of eye, iris colour – dark and light sections matching the direction of the light *Surroundings*: Under eyebrow, below eye 'bags': each area helps shape and tidy the eyes
2. Paint flesh – all	Every figure has different amounts of the following palette: *Base*: Naples Yellow + Napthol Light Red + Brilliant Magenta *Shading*: *1st*: Olive Green + Brilliant Magenta *2nd*: Burnt Sienna + Brilliant Magenta *3rd*: Burnt Umber + Cadmium Orange *Beard*: + Payne's Grey *Highlights*: *1st*: Vallejo Light Skintone for eyes and highest highlights *2nd*: Naples Yellow + Vallejo Dark Cadmium Red *Final touch for each face*: Soft shadows on cheeks with VCadmium Umber Red
3. Paint hair: Henri and Léon	Henri: *Base*: Burnt Umber *Shadows*: Olive Green + Cadmium Orange *Highlights*: VLight Skintone + Cadmium Orange Léon: *Base*: Burnt Sienna + Olive Green *Shadow*: Burnt Umber *Highlight*: Base + Naples Yellow Each layer includes Vallejo Mecha Satin Varnish to give more sheen to the hair

(Continued)

Continued

Important Steps	Key Points (All paints Jo Sonja unless otherwise stated)
4. Paint 'Green' uniform 1: Henri, the Officer	Jacket: *Base*: Burnt Umber *Shadow and highlights*: Use stippling with mixes of Burnt Umber, Raw Sienna and Naples Yellow Trousers: *Base*: Olive Green + Carbon Black + Raw Umber *Shadow*: Carbon Black + Raw Umber *Highlights*: Base + Naples Yellow Inner leg: *Base*: Raw Umber *Shadow*: MSP Oiled Leather + Naples Yellow *Highlights*: Naples Yellow Belt: *Base*: Cadmium Orange + Citadel Rhinox Hide + Vallejo Mecha Satin Varnish *Shadow*: Rhinox Hide + Game Colour Smokey Hue *Highlight*: Cadmium Orange Gaiters: *Base*: MSP Oiled Leather Boots: *Base*: AK3Gen Brit Khaki *Shadow*: VBlack + Smokey Hue *Highlights*: VField Grey
5. Paint 'Green' uniform 2: Léon	Jacket and trousers: as per Henri Puttees: *Base*: AK 3Gen Brit Uniform, *Shadow*: + Raw Umber *Highlights*: + Naples Yellow Boots: *Base*: VField Grey *Shadow*: VBlack + Game Colour Smokey Hue *Highlights*: VField Grey + Naples Yellow
6. Paint Lancers' caps and jackets	* Top learning is that 'black is not black': rather, it is a combination of darker grey tones with a primary tint. * The primary tint for caps was a warm reddish tone using Raw Sienna mixed with Prussian Blue. * The tint for jackets was a greenish blue with Raw Umber base, then Prussian Blue with Burnt Umber. * The deepest shadow in the seams and inside sleeves was emphasized with thinned washes of W&N Lamp Black oil paint. **Note:** For further guidance when painting black do search out Swedish master modeller Mike Blank's 'Black and White' articles and books. He has made an art form of painting these colours for many years.

(Continued)

Continued

Important Steps	Key Points (All paints Jo Sonja unless otherwise stated)
7. Paint Lancers' grey trousers	*Base*: Payne's Grey *Shadow*: Payne's Grey + Burnt Umber *Alternative*: Replace Umber with Prussian Blue to give a cleaner, blue tinge rather than grubby, weathered tone *Highlight*: Nimbus Grey Paint was stippled with a fine brush, then cross-hatching was used with alternating stripes of shadow and highlight creasing across their laps, from hours of sitting and driving Minervas. Leg stripes: *Base*: Raw Umber *Yellow – base*: Turners Yellow; *shadow*: Raw Umber; *highlight*: Naples Yellow *White – base*: Naples Yellow; *shadow*: Raw Umber; *highlight*: Warm White Leather cuffs: *Base*: CSnakebite Leather *Shadow*: CRhinox Hide with deep shadow Smokey Hue *Highlights*: Base + VSaddle Brown Shoes: *Base*: VMatt Black *Shadow*: CAbaddon Black *Highlights*: Raw Sienna + Raw Umber
8. Paint Lancers' detail and equipment	Kepi: *Base*: Raw Umber *Highlight*: Bright Magenta + Naples Yellow *Shadow*: Carbon Black Goggles strap: *Base*: Olive Green *Shadow*: Carbon Black *Highlight*: Base + Naples Yellow *Red trim*: *Base*: Napthol Crimson *Highlight* 1: Napthol Red Light *Highlight* 2: Cadmium Orange Brim: Satin Varnish + Burnt Umber/Olive Green *Edge*: Satin Varnish + Carbon Black *Highlight*: Satin + Burnt Umber + Naples Yellow

Flesh paint colours for this figure group included new primary tones: Magenta, Olive Green and French Blue.

(Left to right) *Léon, Henri, Pierre, Étienne, Thierry : 1:35 Belgians painted for Copper State Models to accompany their Minerva and Lanchester armoured car models.*

Red is added to the eyes (left) to represent tiredness, and the face is finished with lighter colours (right) to represent a pale complexion.

Minerva driver c.1916 from the 1st Lancers, with chamois-lined trousers and gaiters instead of puttees.
HENK DEVOS

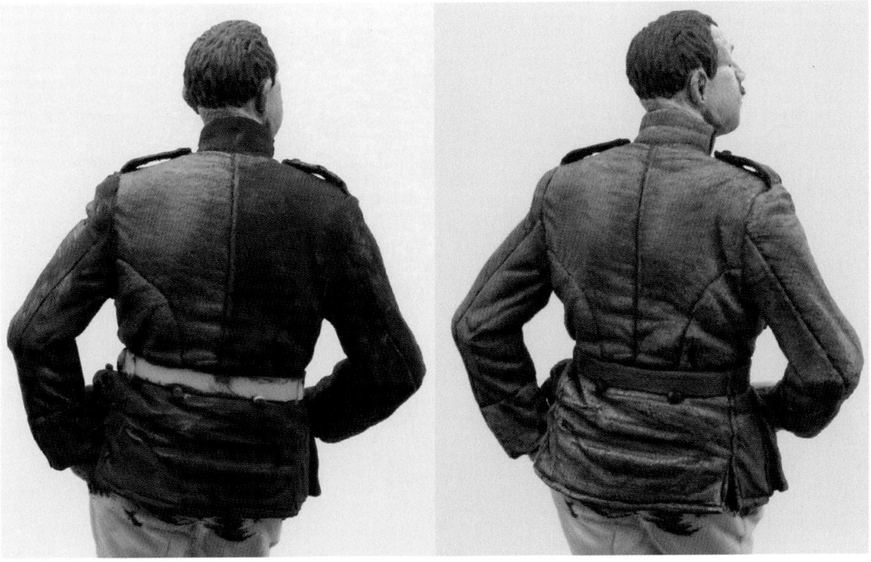

Start on the back left side (left), then the right back (right), then the front right with sleeve, then left front and left sleeve. Alternatively work from the top down the front, then the back sides.

It is possible to be too pedantic when doing textures: most importantly aim for tone consistency across each panel.

Léon looks tidier, with leather gaiters and boots – each differ in black tones. There is a covered helmet in the kit for his bare head.

Henri has small features such a strap made from insulation tape, missing buttons, and his pocket and epaulettes have lifted.

A Minerva driver c.1914 from the 1st Lancers, with kepi and goggles, grabs a meal from his mug.
HENK DEVOS

Bluish-grey trousers using Payne's Grey (left) as a base on Thierry, plus a second coat and Snakebite Leather (right) as a base for the reinforced cuffs.

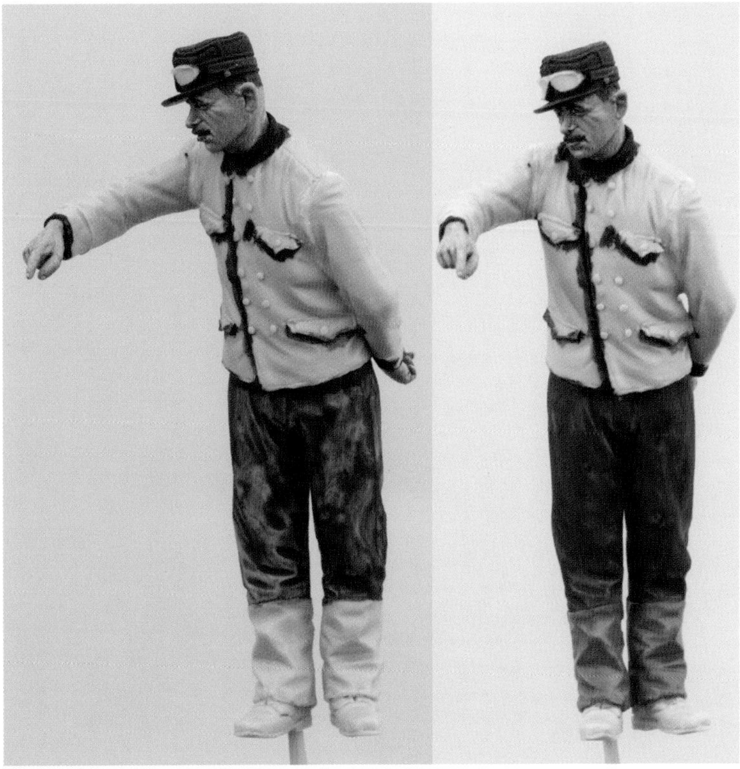

Pierre shows heavily creased and worn trousers from the hours spent driving his armoured car. This version is still fairly rough – the final version is blended a little more.

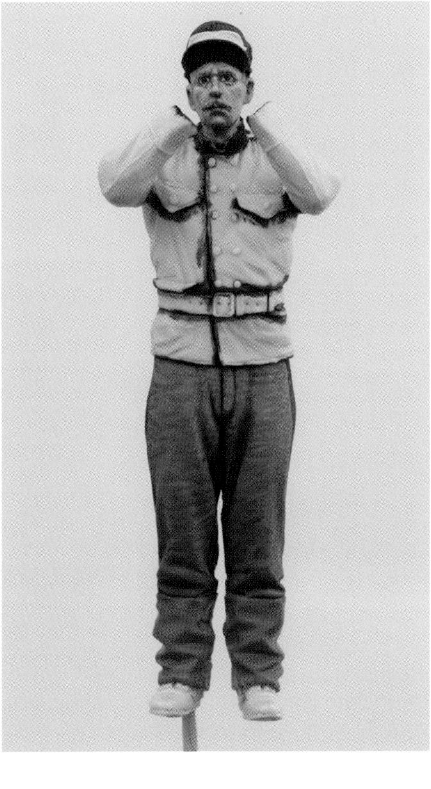

Étienne's trousers have a faded look (left), and yellow (right) also makes them look lighter. Note the piping should be white or blue with a narrow stripe between broad stripes.

Thierry pointing, Étienne checking his map, and Pierre surveying the route ahead with his binoculars: a 'brave little Belgium' Minerva crew.

Tip

* If acrylics dry with an unsatisfactory sheen, either mix them with a more reliable matt paint such as a Jo Sonja, or add a small amount of Tamiya X-21 Flat Base to a blending or glaze medium. Then use this mix to thin and apply the paint. Be careful not to overuse Flat Base as it will result in paints drying with a chalky effect.
* Special brushes are not required for the different acrylics effects, but it is helpful to have a separate set for oils. This set should be washed regularly with washing-up liquid and warm water, as these brushes become contaminated by oils.
* Brighten up a figure by adding personal items such as a tartan scarf, knitted socks, a spotted handkerchief, a sun flap or a coloured pullover from home. Troops would often wear non-standard items to stay cool or warm.

PAINTING FRENCH

Painting Aviateurs d'Escadrons

French pilots and aircrew were as colourfully dressed as they were colourful in life. CSM produce a series of these 1:32 French Aéronautique Militaire figures to go with their Nieuport and Caudron G.III aircraft. Four figures are used here – Antonin, Raoul, Claude and Didier, a French aircrew from 1916–18 – to demonstrate methods of painting the colours associated with the French World War I aviators' red, black, tan and Bleu Horizon uniforms. (Although expressed as 'Horizon Blue' in English, the French term is used throughout this book.)

Major Felix 'Antonin' Brocard was one of the most senior French pilots, building his flying reputation initially as a commander of the premier 'Storks' escadrilles (squadrons). After being shot through the jaw, he went on to become renowned for recruiting and training exceptional talent, such as the most famous of French aviators, Georges Guynemer.

As a highly influential leader he was also given command of other units, including Escadrille de

It was enjoyable trying to mimic miniature textures and get them looking realistic, as Raoul's uniform in the first attempt at recreating Bleu Horizon.

Three figures, grouped in a balanced triangular arrangement, with varying heights, is aesthetically pleasing. Furniture and equipment fills the void between each character.

Many soldiers became airmen as war progressed. Initially wearing their army uniform, like Claude and Didier, another multicoloured option is René, a Wings Cockpit figure.

La Fayette N.124. This unit was made up of French and ex-pat US pilots. Amongst these was the eccentric Major Gervais 'Raoul' Lufbery, a dual ace who served with both French and US air forces. A sign of Lufbery's bizarre style, he doted on a pair of pet lion cubs called 'Whiskey' and 'Soda' during his flying career. Raoul was an earlier CSM project, a simpler palette being used to paint his blue French uniform.

In the vignette shared here, Antonin is joined by a couple of his team in 1917 watching the squadron return home. Relaxing smoking a pipe is a veteran soldier 'Didier', turned pilot sergeant major. He wears a turtleneck jumper, popular with French pilots such as Brocard, and a plain black jacket as Guynemer, partly covered by his aviator overalls. Meanwhile, newly recruited Sous-Lieutenant 'Claude' sips his coffee in his stylish artillery uniform, proudly displaying his freshly received 1916 pilot wings and military medal. Painting different tones of Bleu Horizon to get it right can be a challenge, so it is worth thinking a little more about this colour (*see* 'Painting It Right' later in this chapter).

Painting the Key Points of Raoul

Important Steps	Key Points: Raoul (All paints Jo Sonja unless otherwise stated)
1. Paint face and hands	*Base*: VBeige Red + Raw Sienna *Highlight*: Naples Yellow *Shadows*: Burnt Sienna and VCadmium Umber Red
2. Paint turtleneck	*Shadow*: Carbon Black + Hookers Green *Highlight*: Naples Yellow
3. Paint kepi	*Shadow*: Carbon Black + Prussian Green *Highlight*: Naples Yellow *Trim*: Titanium White *Brim*: VBlack *Metal*: VGold + VSilver
4. Paint uniform	*Base*: Carbon Black *Jacket and trouser*: Done using AK WWI French Uniforms Paint Set in sequence, dark to light: 1. Shadow 2. Base 3. Light *Puttees*: Same shadow and base from the AK set, the only change being that Naples Yellow was used as a highlight *Red tabs*: Napthol Crimson
5. Paint belt and shoes	*Base*: Raw Sienna *Shadow*: VBlack+ Satin Varnish *Worn toes and belt highlight:* Naples Yellow
6. Paint badges and medals	*Collar wings*: VSilver + Raw Umber shade *Légion d'honneur*: *Red ribbon*: Burgundy; *Enamel*: Sap Green, Pearl White, Rich Gold *Military medal*: Ribbon Sap Green, Yellow Light; VSilver outer, + Paynes Gray, VGold *Croix de guerre*: Ribbon: Napthol Red Light, Sap Green + Naples Yellow; *Medal*: VBrass

Raoul was first painted as a French flier, so a simplified palette was used for his flesh and an AK paint set for his uniform.

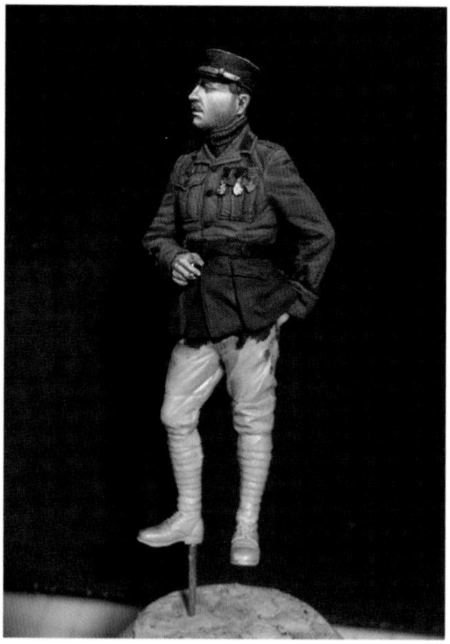

Raoul and Antonin both have etched brass medals, which needed research to get the ribbon colours correct; they add a spot of colour to their uniforms.

Turtleneck pullovers were popular with French pilots, and particular attention was made to paint the ribbing on this.

A couple of years elapsed between painting Raoul and the other three figures. The evolution in learning and research is evident in the changes made to the palette tested on Antonin and his team.

Creating Characters – Painting Faces

Personally I find it a new challenge to land every face, especially as I try to capture what's in my mind. Every one of my figures has a name, so it has a personality that I'll try to represent. I have to remind myself to 'trust the process' and keep working until a smile or a twinkle in the eye appears. Character for me comes from the eyes, with shadow and light around them. The face surrounding the eyes is also important as it helps frame them. Light and shadow around the mouth help reinforce a look or an expression. This can be achieved using various paints and techniques with different textures and materials. The challenge is always to know when to stop!

Painting the Key Points of All Three Figures

Important Steps	Key Points: All Three Figures (All Paints Jo Sonja Unless Otherwise Stated)
1. Paint flesh and hair	*Base*: Skintone Base Shadow: 1. Yellow Oxide + brown (Burnt Sienna or Brown Earth) + green (Sap Green or Pine Green) 2. Cadmium Orange + green + brown 3. Neck shading: Napthol Crimson + Cadmium Orange + Sap Green + Burnt Sienna *Beard area*: Cadmium Orange + Ultramarine Blue *Highlights*: 1. Yellow Oxide + Cadmium Orange 2. Naples Yellow + Skintone Base *Red tones*: cheeks, lips, ears; *nose tip*: Napthol Crimson + Burgundy Hair: *Antonin*: dark – *base*: Burnt Umber; *highlight*: Burnt Sienna + Yellow Oxide *Claude*: blonde – *base*: Raw Umber; *shadow*: Burnt Sienna + Hookers Green; *highlight*: Naples Yellow *Didier*: light brown – *base*: Brown Earth; *shadow*: Burnt Sienna; *highlight*: Cadmium Orange + Naples Yellow *Key Points*: *Antonin*
2. Paint kepi	Red – *base*: Napthol Red Light; *shadow*: Napthol Crimson; *highlight*: Cadmium Orange Black – *base*: Carbon Black; *highlight*: Provincial Beige + Payne's Grey *Brim*: VBlack + Satin Varnish Gold trim – *base*: Raw Sienna or Yellow Oxide; *shadow*: Burnt Umber + VSmokey Ink; *highlight*: Rich Gold
3. Paint uniform	*Base*: Payne's Grey *White collar*: Warm White Jacket: *Shadow*: AK WWI French Uniform Shadow + MSP Ritterlich Blue *Highlight*: 1. Naples Yellow; 2. + Artelier Pastel Arctic Blue Trousers: *Shadow*: Payne's Grey *Highlights*: Artelier Dioxazine Purple + Naples Grey *Stripe*: Yellow Oxide + Naples Yellow Puttees: *Base*: Carbon Black *Main*: AK WWI French Uniform Base *Highlight*: + Naples Yellow
4. Paint fur coat	*Coat lining*: Provincial Beige + Yellow Oxide, VNew Wood Fur: *Base*: Alizarin Crimson + Burnt Umber, *Highlight 1*: Raw Sienna + Ultramarine Blue *Highlight 2*: Warm White + Raw Sienna

(*Continued*)

Continued

Important Steps	Key Points: All Three Figures (All paints Jo Sonja unless otherwise stated)
5. Paint shoes	*Polished leather upper*: Burnt Umber, VBlack *Leather sole*: Raw Umber
6. Paint medals and badges	*Collar wings*: Golden Iridescent Bronze *Légion d'honneur and Croix de guerre*: as Raoul **Note:** Rosette added from a foil disc made with a jewellers' awl

All three figures used the same flesh palette, but it was still possible to vary the mixes, giving each a different skin tone.

The next stage in painting each face of the trio was to build up shadows using Da Vinci 2/0 and 10/0 brushes.

Claude has an air about him, and the aim was to bring this out, starting with outlining the eyes, nose and mouth.

Lighter shadows are blended in to soften the upper face, while greying under the mouth develops the lower face structure.

Antonin has a mature face with the wearied look of a commander worried about his men; highlighting around the eyes and mouth heightens this expression.

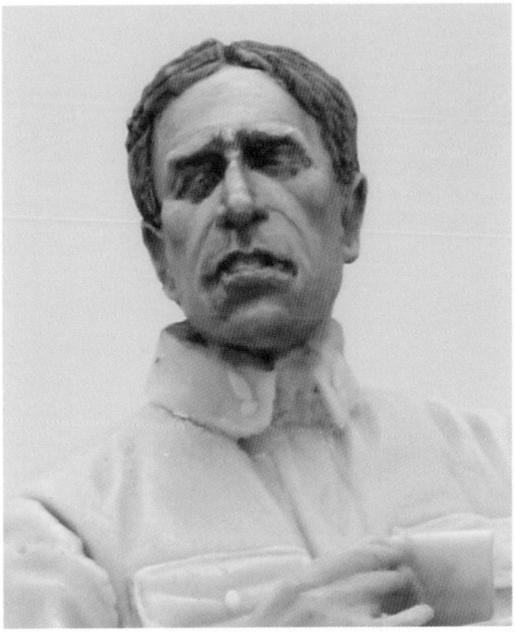

Breaking the rule of completing the eyes before doing the rest of the face strangely gave a certain freedom in painting Claude's features across his 'red zone' cheeks, nose and lips.

The full painting set-up, including a more extensive Bleu Horizon palette trialled for this group of pilots.

The kepi just needs a metallic trim, then on to the white collar effect, painted above a Payne's Grey base coat. The dash of light blue on the puttees was a colour test.

Before completing the fur coat a patchy acrylic undercoat is flowed into all the sculpted fur detail.

Separate legs allow the inside of the fur coat to be painted, before finishing a brighter and lighter jacket using another experimental colour mix.

Thickened oil paints have been daubed on the fur coat, giving a lushness and strong contrast of surfaces to the matt blues of the uniform.

Painting the Key Points of Claude

Important Steps	Key Points: Claude (All paints Jo Sonja unless otherwise stated)
1. Paint uniform	Jacket and Kepi: AK WWI French Uniform Blue base + VAndrea Blue *Shadow*: Payne's Grey *Deep Shadow*: + Raw Umber *Highlight*: Artelier Arctic Blue Trousers: As Didier's jacket *Stripe*: Napthol Red Crimson and Red Light
2. Paint gaiters and boots	*Base*: VBurnt Orange *Shadows*: Burnt Sienna + Satin Varnish *Highlight*: Brown Earth + Provincial Beige
3. Paint accessories	*Table and chair*: VBurnt Orange *Shadow*: + Raw Umber + Satin Varnish *Highlight*: VBurnt Orange *Dust*: Provincial Beige and scuffs from Citadel Bleached Bone *Cup and saucer*: VGloss White; *coffee*: VSmokey Ink *Cane*: CRhinox Hide

With the flesh now complete it was time to base coat the clothing items. Check out a minor modification: a raised 'pinkie' on the hand holding the cup.

Claude looks up from his coffee to watch the fighters returning from patrol. The chair, table and walking stick have a polished wood effect.

Painting the Key Points of Didier

Important Steps	Key Points: Didier (All paints Jo Sonja unless otherwise stated)
1. Paint kepi	Carbon Black + Payne's Grey Light: + Warm White Dark: Carbon Black *Brim*: VBlack edge + Provincial Beige + SatinV
2. Paint jacket	*Undercoat*: Carbon Black *Shadow*: 1. Midnite Blue 2. + Carbon Black 3. + Burnt Sienna + Raw Umber + Carbon Black *Dirt smears*: Provincial Beige
3. Paint overalls	*Base*: Provincial Beige *Shadows*: Raw Umber + Burnt Umber *Highlight*: Turners Yellow + Naples Yellow
4. Paint shoes	*Base*: Raw Sienna *Shadows*: Burnt Umber + Satin Varnish *Highlight*: Turners Yellow
5. Paint pipe	*End and cap*: VSilver *Shaft*: Raw Sienna + Satin Varnish *Highlight*: CBleached Bone

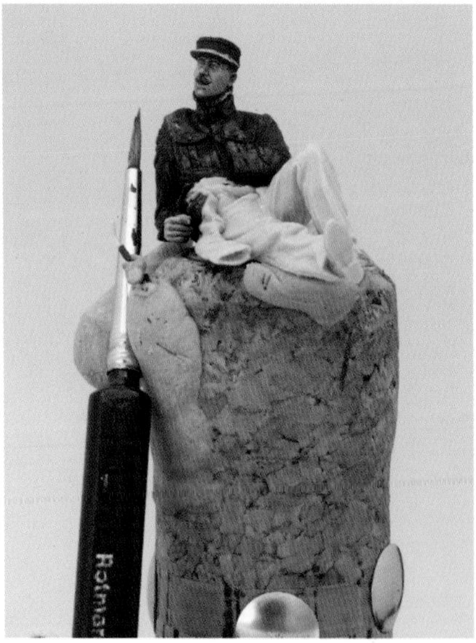

Didier mounted on a cork for painting, with Blu Tack supporting his extended leg. An old Size 1 brush was used to undercoat his uniform.

The tunic is completed with a gold trim undercoat, then on to underpainting the overalls; the lower section is roughly shaded with a dark base coat.

The finished effect on Didier; a different complexion has been achieved compared to his fellow aviators, as well as hand and pipe detailing.

Painting It Right

What does 'painting it right' actually mean? When thinking about painting uniforms, one point to remember is that colours vary greatly. Actual

From behind the variation can be seen between the darker tunic and the tan overalls, brown leather shoes, white turtleneck and the gold lace on the kepi.

uniform examples shared in this book are intended to show colour variations for the French World War I uniform hue called Bleu Horizon, and in other chapters the British Khaki Drab. All references we have are over 100 years old, whether they be colour photographs, or period uniform examples. All will show signs of ageing from light exposure. Colours fade over time, so unless access to a museum stocked with actual examples is readily available, only an informed judgement of the actual colour can be made based upon best references.

Remember, too, that when photographed or reproduced online, colours are affected by the tone of the reprinted or virtual image, as well as other variables such as the colour of ink used, and the light tone in which the photo was taken and developed. Think also about the effect that backgrounds can have, as also materials or equipment displayed around the uniforms. Then there is the type of material, how it has been dyed, where it has been worn, how it has been stored... All of this will affect the way the colour is viewed and interpreted by the eyes and mind.

It is therefore almost impossible to land on exactly the right colour when painting uniform fabric. All efforts will be what the modeller interprets as correct to them. Options to help check 'what looks right' include sharing photos online, showing work-in-progress images, asking for second and third opinions. Even these, however, are still also opinions, not facts. If in real doubt, or if there are concerns about this, it is possible to reach out to experts in the field on specialist forums such as the Great War Forum or Forum Militaria 14/18.

One way to avoid these painting dilemmas is simply to use pre-mix acrylics such as AK Interactive's World War I French or British Uniform Colours, or the LifeColor World War I British set. These are useful starters and do yield satisfactory results. However, as confidence grows, and to get more of the natural variety, it is helpful to explore other mixes, such as those shared in the painting notes for these projects.

French Adrian Steel Helmets

The photo and table below show a selection of original World War I French model 1915 Adrian steel helmets from the collection of Yannick Olivères.

Adrian helmets.

Adrian Steel Helmets

Position	Key Points
1. Left	* Infantry helmet manufactured by the firm Léon Delmas. * Front rim buckled – the same effect is attempted with the 'François' bust. * Note the difference in paint finish: this helmet and the engineer's on the right have a darker coat of paint, referred to as 'Midnight Blue'. * This darker, hand-applied coat was implemented on helmets in the field due to a 1916 order instructing poilus to cover the earlier, brighter Bleu Horizon factory finish with a more muted tone for better concealment. (Poilu means 'hairy', a French term of endearment for common soldiers due to their bushy moustaches and longer haircuts.)
2. Front centre	* Artillery helmet with crossed cannons behind a flaming grenade badge. * From 'Dupeyron', with Bleu Horizon factory paint. * Helmet crest combs all varied slightly, due to the manufacturer; the comb was not for decoration, but was intended to act as a shock absorber. * The paint is scratched and scraped back to the steel base.
3. Back centre	* Infantry helmet from 'Le Jouet De Paris'. * This poilu owner has scratched his signature, 'Boisclair', in the right side of his helmet. * Factory-applied, duller Bleu Horizon paint coat. * Rim riveted on the sides; the original Adrian maker 'Japy' welded this seam.
4. Right	* Engineer's badge on the helmet from the firm 'Dupeyron'. * 'Midnight Blue' has been painted over the factory coat by the poilu. * Leather chin straps pulled over the front rim, with square brass/metal adjuster.

French Uniforms: Officers and Poilus

Item	Key Points – Source: Tim
1. Three-quarter trousers	105th heavy artillery regiment, with red piping
2. Tailor-made officer's jacket	* Second lieutenant 74th infantry regiment * Worn from 1916 to the end of the war * Upper left sleeve four frontline line service = 2.5 years of frontline service stripes, called 'sardines' by poilus
3. Official type 1914 jacket with tailor modification	* Sergeant 105th heavy artillery regiment * Worn mid-1915 to the end of the war * Tailor modified (chest pockets added) * Service stripes for two years – one for the first year, then another for each six months afterwards. Introduced in July 1916
4. Official type 1915 jacket and kepi	* 159th infantry regiment soldier * Worn mid-1915 to the end of the war * Standard kepi has a leather peak; it may have the unit number on the front crown, above the chinstrap
5. Tailor-made NCO jacket	* Sergeant 78th infantry regiment * Worn from 1916 to the end of the war * 2 x shoulder stripes for eighteen months frontline service
6. Official type 1915 greatcoat	* 159th infantry regiment * Although designed in 1915, not seen before June 1916, and worn till the end of the war

Actual Bleu Horizon uniforms.

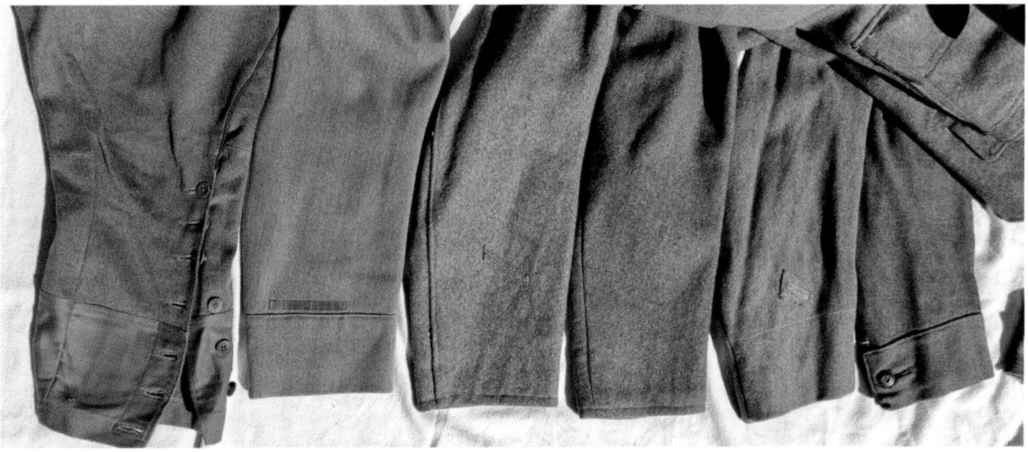

Cuff detail on the uniforms.

Painting French Soldiers

The French began the war in their dark blue jackets and bright red trousers, but like the Belgians, it wasn't long before these were confirmed as being well past their 'use by' date. Instead, troops began to purchase either new khaki trousers, or to be issued the latest in French camouflage – the light blue-grey coloured uniform known as 'Bleu Horizon' by the soldiers (*see* box 'Historical Note' below).

The figure for this project is a 1:24 75mm ModelCellar French lieutenant called 'Maurice', a

French colonial officer from 1916, one of a duo sculpted by leading French sculptor Greg Girault. He connects cleverly with an interlocking trench background with 'Louis', a colonial poilu. This latest figure would become yet another experiment, this time trialling the ScaleColour Acrylic Flesh set, plus a 'home-brew' Bleu Horizon palette and the chance to produce an accurate-looking section of earth trench line.

More on Painting Bleu Horizon

After attempting this colour on the French aircrew, some refinement was made when painting Maurice. The greatcoat is a key part of this figure, and the project offered the chance to show it dirtier, consistent with his trench environment. A combination of AK World War I French colour was again used for mid-colours, supplemented by Jo Sonja for deeper shadow and highest light tone. The coat was painted in a systematic way, working in sections from the collar down through the torso, then the sleeves,

Practice, Practice, Practice: A Message for Texturing and Painting

Author's Note: Maurice is one of the final figures I completed before drafting the manuscript for this book. When painting Maurice, the texturing and effects, particularly on his greatcoat, took many hours to achieve. But it is just as valuable to try to paint detail right, as it is to decide when to stop and move on. After all, it is only through repeated practice that learning happens, and certainly in my earlier modelling days I took months to complete a 1:32 scale figure, always desperately trying to get it right. Swedish Master Modeller Mike Blank advised me that you only achieve improvement with new projects. We are our own worst critic, so there are always things we would like to have done better, or achieved differently. See the chapters on Vic and Charlie, where in one case, fixing the mistake was too late, and in the other, feedback was received early enough to sort the problem out successfully.

French heavy artillerymen make ready a large-calibre shell. Again, a wide variety of uniforms and head dresses are worn, including berets, kepis and helmets. OLIVÈRES COLLECTION

A French 6th Colonials crew manning their Hotchkiss M1914 heavy machine gun; they are instantly recognizable by their collar tabs and the anchor under the helmet badge. OLIVÈRES COLLECTION

We learned from previous attempts that AK's French World War I paint set needed more highlights for a lighter blue/grey effect, so added Jo Sonja.

and down to the skirt. Particular effort was made to be less conservative in painting the light/dark tones to give this a more obvious effect, yet not too extreme that it detracted from its authentic appearance when placed against the darker trench background.

The dilemma when painting uniforms is that we often have to work from photos for colours and representation of materials. Sharing 'in progress' photos with others who are more familiar with the actual look and can give first-hand advice is particularly helpful. For this project there were three Francophile enthusiasts helping out. This was invaluable, as their comments helped encourage the project forwards. The way that light, shadow or gloom plays on surfaces reflects a variety that takes much processing. This is one such project, and Bleu Horizon one such colour.

A large painting handle holds the figure secure in a tall jar, while uniform blue paints are prepared on a moist wet palette.

Historical Note: The Bleu Horizon Uniform Colour

The following observations are contained in a translation from a French soldier's letter home:

'Up to twelve or fifteen hundred metres, the hue of the new uniform merges with the horizon, hence the nickname of 'blue horizon' that we are beginning to give it. At closer distances, and up to about six or seven hundred metres, its uniformly grey tone makes it very difficult to appreciate at any distance. With the oxidation suppression of the reflection of metal buttons, or the use of corozo [brown wooden] buttons, nothing will detect the presence of our skirmishers any more.'

SOURCE: FORUM 14-18

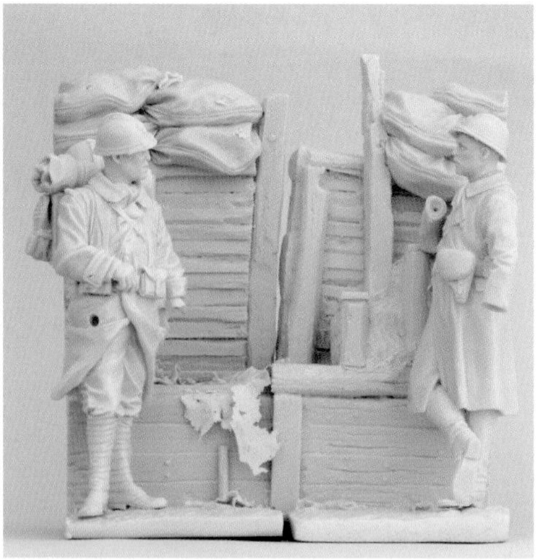

ModelCellar produce this pair on matching trench sections. Torn scraps and debris made from epoxy putty add interest.

Preparing resin kits generally requires removing casting blocks; instead this kit came cleanly cast, only needing holes to be drilled for pins to mount on the base.

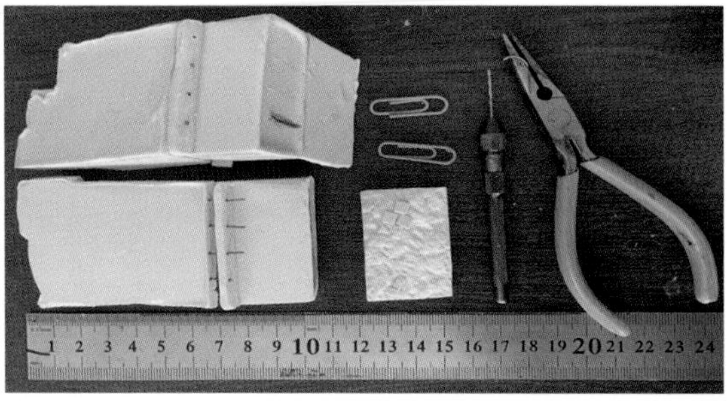

Each base has three parts, their joints strengthened by drilling and by gluing in pins cut from paperclips with epoxy glue.

A painting handle, bought from Mike Sewell at EuroMilitaire 2018, is used to support the larger 75mm figure versus the overbalanced poilu on cork.

Painting Maurice

Important Steps	Key Points (All paints Jo Sonja unless otherwise stated SC = Scale75 ScaleColour Flesh paint set)
1. Paint face	*Base*: Skintone Base *Eyes*: VLight Flesh, Carbon Black, Payne's Grey Shadow: 1. SCBurnt Skin + SCMoss Green 2. SCGolden Flesh + Prussian Blue *Highlight*: 1. SCGolden Flesh + Pink Flesh 2. Light Flesh 3. VLight Flesh for nose tip and brow Beard: *Base*: Prussian Blue *Shadow*: SCGreen, SCRed - Heavier Red as wash with grey tone as base for beard area *Highlight*: SCLight Flesh *See* photo 'Step by Step' for further explanation.
2. Paint écharpe (scarf)	*Base*: Carbon Black *Stripe Pattern*: Deco 3D Texture paint used to add ribbing in thin layers *Dark Stripes*: SCMoss Green from Flesh Set *Highlight*: Naples Yellow to emphasize the effect of faded wool dyes and generally messy cloth
3. Paint casque (helmet)	*Base*: Humbrol Matt Oxford Blue *Weathering*: Mig Distressed Paint medium covered with a Light Blue mix (MSP Ritterlich Blue + Andrea Blue + Raw Umber) * Finished with Vallejo light grey and blue washes mixed with Satin varnish. * The aim is to depict heavy wear, silt and a muddied effect on a well-used helmet. **Note:** The colonial troops anchor symbol below the flaming grenade badge on the helmet front was added from Deco acrylic texture paint.
4. Paint capote (greatcoat)	*Base*: Raw Umber *Shadow*: AK French Shadow + Raw Umber **Note:** The shading on the right side below the shoulder and down below the binoculars is heavier due to shadowing of the trench wall. Highlight: 1. AKFrench WWI Base + SkinTone Base 2. AK French WWI Light Weathering: 1. Burnt Umber stibbled into light and shadow during stippling 2. Dried mud a mix of Naples Yellow + Raw Sienna **Note:** It was found to be necessary to prepare AK World War I French Blue Base by letting it settle overnight on a wet palette before use. Early tests confirmed

(Continued)

Continued

Important Steps	Key Points (All paints Jo Sonja unless otherwise stated SC = Scale75 ScaleColour Flesh paint set)
	that if used too soon directly out of the bottle it had a more purple hue, and over time this tended to a greener hue. This colour variation was not helpful when trying to texture the larger greatcoat surface area over many painting sessions, but was fine on smaller projects such as Raoul earlier.
5. Paint leather	* All were painted over a solid base of MSP Burnt Orange (BO). * Each set of colours was blended and dabbed on with splashes or washes using Vallejo Mecha Satin Varnish; this helped give transparency to the layers and resulted in an obvious sheen. Belt and cross-strap: *Shadow*: LCBrit Uniform Dark Leather *Highlight*: VOrange Brown + MSP Burnt Orange * The back cross-belt is well sculpted, with the greatcoat bunched up under it. After feedback online this was emphasized with a deep shadow using Carbon Black. Binoculars case: *Shadow*: SCMoss Green + SCCrimson; *Highlight*: VOrange Brown Pistol holster: *Shadow*: 1. SCCrimson + VOrange Brown; 2. + SCMoss Green *Highlight*: VOrange Brown Boots: *Base*: 1. Carbon Black; 2. VOrange Brown smeared on *Glaze*: VBlack thinned with Satin Varnish dabbed on leaving VOrange Brown exposed * Mud was built up from the groundwork texture and painted using the same washes to blend into the earth
6. Paint brass	* The main effort here is to show a slight variation between the dull, tarnished brass buckles, buttons and rings. This is achieved with a couple of mixes that both use Citadel Zambesi Desert as the base colour, Vallejo Satin Varnish and Glazing Medium to blend, and are then finished with an overcoat of Game Colour (GC) Green Shade Wash to kill the brightest of the brass tones: *Mix 1 – Shade*: GCSmokey Ink + Vallejo Brass; *highlights*: Brass + Golden Fluid Iridescent Bronze (a particularly fine, soft tone useful for light on yellow metals) *Mix 2 – Shade*: GCSmokey Ink + P3 Brass Balls; *highlight*: P3 Brass Balls
7. Attach hands	* Each hand was mounted on paperclips and the cuffs drilled out. * They were painted separately, as each had a fragile component – a pipe and a cane. * These were left off until all set to mount on the base, then slower-drying thick superglue was added to the pin end, and each was twisted into place.

(*Continued*)

Continued

Important Steps	Key Points (All paints Jo Sonja unless otherwise stated SC = Scale75 ScaleColour Flesh paint set)
8. Construct and finish the base	* Each part of the base was cleaned up and assembled with paper clips to reinforce the main joint, and glued with two-part Araldite adhesive. * It was then over-sprayed with Citadel's Zandri Dust. * Each section was base coated with a variety of tones: *Sandbags*: VGreen Ochre *Moist ground*: GC Earth *Wood*: Vallejo Old and New Wood colours for slight variety (though most of this will be lost with wash and weathering) *Trench earth and woodwork*: Primarily done with AK products (*see* photos).

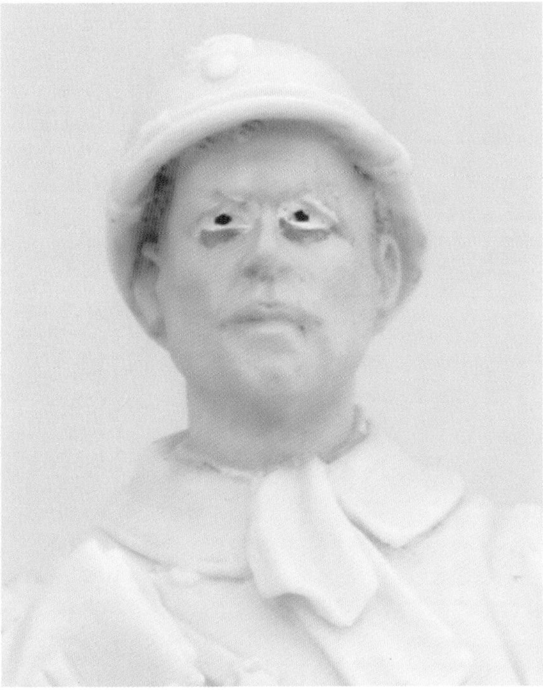

Face 1: Undercoated with a base Skintone, then light pink for the eyes, followed by carefully positioned dark spots for the irises.

Face 2: The deepest shadow is shaped around the eyes, nostrils, upper lip, ear and under the chin, then mid-shadow tones under the helmet, temples and over the cheeks.

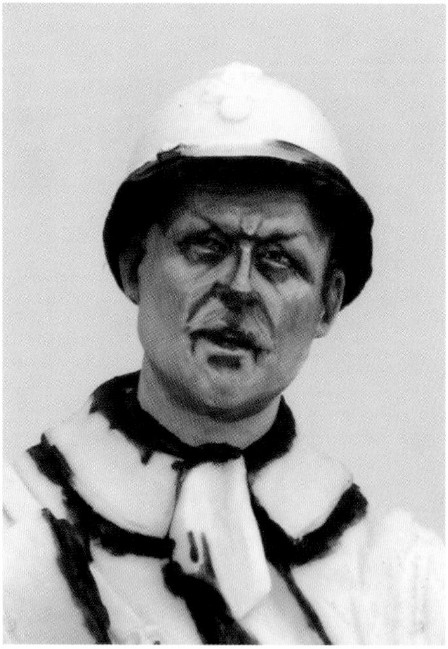

Face 3: More focused work to bring together the 'yellow zone' parts at the top of the face, including the furrowed brow and the upper eye area.

Although the eyes are the focal point for any face, they are only part of the story: be sure to put as much effort into the area surrounding the eyes, too.

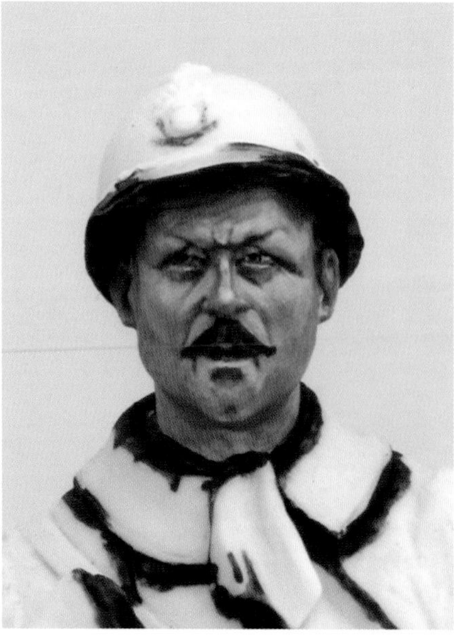

Face 4: In the 'red zone' pinker tones are added around the mid part of the face below the eyes and above the 'blue zone' where a start is being made to stipple on the beard.

Colonial units had an anchor under their helmet grenade badge. This was made using Deco 3D paint, as on the scarf.

Acrylics offer a wide range of different mediums, such as this thickened acrylic texture paint, useful to create detail effects.

Bleu 1: Rough wash of AK Uniform Base over the base – the splotchy effect is OK, though add more on areas that will be highlighted.

A solid Raw Umber undercoat lays the foundation for the Bleu Horizon greatcoat, with a brighter orange hue for leather equipment.

Bleu 2: Stipple and stibble in highlights down the greatcoat and upwards with shadow tones, blending from larger spots to finer ones.

Bleu 3: Texture larger sections by dabbing and stibbling a mid blue-grey third coat, before applying a final finish as on the upper sections.

The greatcoat almost completed, though it will be dirtied further to be consistent with his trench environment. The boots are washed with a leather base.

An iPhone snap gives another perspective. It took many hours to ensure that the greatcoat sections blended together properly, but the end result is worth it.

The hands are drilled and pinned to paint separately, as each holds a fragile item. The boots are given sheen with semi-gloss acrylic.

Almost all done, with the hands and colonial collar insignia painted up. The hands are kept loose until they are finally mounted on to the base.

The aim for this small scene is to complement the figure rather than overpower or detract from him. Louis the Poilu will join later.

A fresh palette prepared with wood and earthen shades to use as a base for sandbags and weathered trench woodwork.

AK groundwork products are enamels, therefore take more cleaning and effort than the usual approach with water-based acrylics.

The first pass over the sprayed woodwork was with AK Brown Wood filter. Note the shrapnel-damaged sandbags that will have sand dribbling from them.

Wood comes to life with thin coats of AK Wood Enamel Wash. Sandbags are given a similar approach with rough coats of Kursk Earth.

Further attention for Maurice's base included streaked earth colours on the woodwork and Dark Earth pigment with Kursk Earth for the sandbags.

Repeat the Enamel Wood wash and more Damp Earth. Pigments and washes take extra care, however the upside is that their realistic, natural finish is hard to beat.

The woodwork was lightened up further with Vallejo acrylics, then a layer of Dark Earth pigment, mixed with Damp Earth, is laid on with coarse brushes.

Earth is carried up on to the boots and greatcoat, as well as over the ground litter – empty cardboard cigarette and ammunition cartons.

PAINTING BRITISH AND COMMONWEALTH

Uniform Changes: What a Difference a Hat can Make...

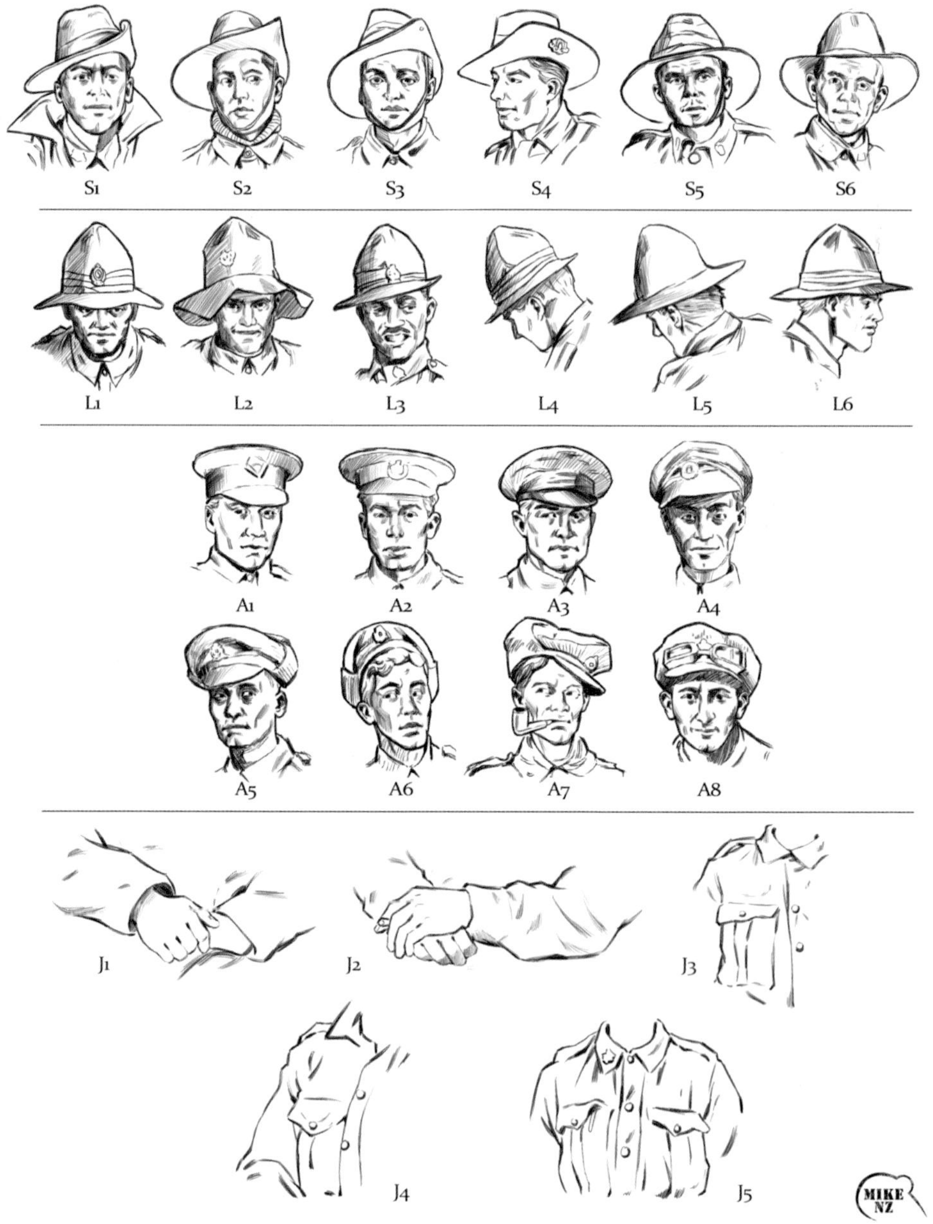

(Continued)

Continued

Study photos and films to see how soldiers really wore their uniforms. Use these to create uniqueness in your figures, with simple small features missed in sculpting or just to add extra character. Every soldier expressed their personality in how they wore their clothing and equipment, not to mention the effect of personal hygiene standards, battle surroundings and weather conditions endured when on campaign. All these factors influence how figures actually looked, in contrast to what regulations may have said. The plates illustrate a number of examples for you to consider when personalizing your own figures and dioramas.

Australian Felt Slouch Hat

(S1–6) Australian solders wore their felt slouch, with its plain felt band, with panache and style. In these examples note the angle of the hat when it is worn up (S1–S3), and the more lateral brim when worn down (S5–S6). Chinstraps were worn on the edge of the chin sometimes, more often on formal occasions or photo shoots (S2, S3) and less frequently when in the field. Maybe this was because these straps were made of thin leather and could snap easily under stress, or simply the hat was more comfortable without the strap. The hat badge was visible when it was folded up (S4).

New Zealand Peaked Felt Hat

(L1–6) The New Zealand troops' peaked felt hat had a three-striped pugaree band (L1) indicating their branch of service (see actual examples in the plate). Unlike Australian hats, New Zealand ones did not have a reinforced rim, so while they may have arrived flat, they were more prone to flopping once they had been wet or out in field (L2). Kiwi soldiers also trimmed the felt brim to make it narrower (L3, L4). The side profile of the peak shows that it was inconsistent in shape, and no two lemon squeezers look identical (L5, L6). Badges were not always present, but could have been lost during action, or taken off and kept in a safe place.

British SD Caps

(A1–8) British Service Dress (SD) Caps came in many styles and were worn in lots of ways. Again, each one tells a story. Upright, well shaped and sharp (A1), a new Maori recruit is proudly photographed before departure with his red/black diagonally patched cap. Tommies on their way to the frontline are depicted wearing a standard issue cap, with its flatter top (A2) or pushed-up peak (A3). When working, chin straps were stashed out of the way over the top of the unit badge (A4). Caps were worn with a crumpled top (A5) when in the line, or pushed up to mop the brow (A6), or askew to avoid knocking the peak on a gun trail or the side of a vehicle being repaired (A7). This version with ear flaps over the top (A5–7) was also known as the 'Gor-Blimey' trench cap. One interesting variation from the khaki serge caps was the same style, but all in tan leather. A tighter-fitting version was issued to despatch riders (A8), whose job demanded a harder-wearing material and because pushing goggles up and down damaged the flimsy cloth caps.

Cuffs, Epaulettes and Pocket Flaps

(J1–5) Cuffs can be carefully scraped open with a sharp-pointed craft knife. Note the difference between the British SD open sleeve (J1) and the tighter-fitting, Australian buttoned cuff (J2). Likewise epaulettes can be hollowed out underneath (J3). Pocket flaps can be easily lifted up (J4) with a sharp knife point, or replaced with putty to show them folded into the pocket, with a fountain pen or pencil clipped inside (J5).

Uniform Colours: New Zealand and British Officer Jackets

Historical Note: Uniform Differences

Actual Allied uniform examples are shared in the 'Uniform Colours' sections. However, all clothing varied in tone, and the photos are intended to help guide painters as to real colours, as well as reassure them that variety is key. Uniform colours varied within a unit as a result of washing and doing different jobs, plus newer recruits were issued different batches and manufacturers' kits. Also look carefully at different styles and the features of each item.

Remember when modelling figures that although there were dress regulations, in real life rules were known to be broken due to wartime expedients and battleground conditions. Thorough research is important, but do watch out for oddities such as an Aussie hat worn by a Fernleaf, or a British utility jacket on an Australian, instead of their home issue service dress. Period photos reveal these hidden clues, which can improve understanding of how to model differences in figure projects – more examples of this are given in a few of the plates.

New Zealand and British Officer Jackets

Manufacturer	Key Points – Source: B. O'Sullivan
1. New Zealand-made jacket	* This Territorial jacket is for a lieutenant in the NZ Army Service Corps. * It has been converted from a 1912-pattern jacket with a closed collar and five-button front, to a jacket with an open collar and four-button front. * It has plaited chevron lace on the shoulders. * Around the waist is an integral belt.
2. British-made with fabric shoulder straps and brass shoulder titles	* This is a Territorial jacket for a lieutenant in the NZ Field Artillery. * Above the left cuff is a brass wound stripe. * It has a full set of service stripes, showing service from 1914 First Echelon (red stripe) through to 1918 (four blue stripes, one per year). * It is identified as belonging to 7/416 Harold Erwin Wright. * Harold left as part of the main body in October 1914 and served on Gallipoli in the Canterbury Mounted Rifles. In 1917 he attended officer cadet school in the UK, and was later commissioned, serving with the NZFA in France.
3. New Zealand-made during World War I, but still in use in the 1920s	* Territorial jacket for a major in the 2nd (South Canterbury) Infantry Regiment. * It has no integral waist belt.

Officers.

Other Ranks.

Officer cuffs.

Other Rank cuffs.

Uniform Colours: New Zealand and British Other Ranks' Jackets

Manufacturer	Key Points – Source: B. O'Sullivan
1. New Zealand-made	* First issued in 1912, based on the British 1902 pattern service dress jacket. * The jacket was produced from 1912–1916, and featured the coloured arm of the service braid around the shoulder straps. This colour matched that of the trousers, pantaloons and puggaree (hat band) – here red for infantry. * The official colour of the fabric was 'drab'. * Generally jackets were shorter in the body, and sleeves reached to the low hem of the skirt (unlike the British-made jackets). * These jackets were worn in New Zealand, then by the main body on Gallipoli (until worn out), and should be included when depicting scenes of the landing on 25 April.
2. New Zealand-made private purchase	* Made from drab tweed fabric (officer quality). * This example belonged to 48991 Trooper Joseph F. Mckee, NZMR, 28th Reinforcements. He left New Zealand in June 1917 and served with the 15th Company of the Imperial Camel Corps in Palestine; in July 1918 he was posted to the 2nd NZMG Squadron.

(Continued)

Continued

Manufacturer	Key Points – Source: B. O'Sullivan
3. British-made Other Ranks service dress (SD)	* The third version of the 1902 pattern. The fabric is a rough serge in a drab, but much browner colour. * Badged to a lance corporal in the 2nd Battalion NZRB (black squares). * This jacket had blackened metal collar badges and shoulder titles, and black bakelite buttons. * It had a wound stripe on the lower left cuff.
4. British Other Ranks SD jacket in a different shade of brown drab serge fabric	* 4th Battalion NZRB jacket with an inverted triangle badge on the upper sleeves. * It had blackened badges and bakelite Rifles bugle buttons. * Also worsted corporal stripes and a wound stripe.
5. New Zealand-made jacket in a green drab serge fabric	* Jackets were produced from 1916 to the early World War II period and differ slightly from the earlier New Zealand-made style. * The main difference was that they were made to a higher quality and did not have coloured braid to the edge of the shoulder straps. * Like the earlier New Zealand-made jacket, this one features brass New Zealand Forces 'Southern Cross' buttons.
Note: These jackets are all based on an earlier version, which had over-the-shoulder strapping and pleated top pockets. Another difference was the utility version issued in 1914, which did away with both shoulder straps and pocket pleats.	

Painting World War I Pilots

Author's Note

World War I pilots and aircrew have a special place in history, being the first men to conduct aerial combat. They were the original 'Magnificent Men in Their Flying Machines'. Many were larger-than-life characters, the original aces such as 'The Red Baron' Manfred von Richthofen, Albert Ball, Mick Mannock, Eddie Rickenbacker, Billy Bishop and William Rhodes-Moorhouse VC (*see* 'Historical Note' below). Every one of them personalized their own equipment for the harsh environment of operating in open aircraft cockpits across the skies.

Captain Lanoe Hawker's sad, tired eyes are in contrast with his formal service dress, all ready for parade wearing his ceremonial officer's sword.

The figure in this project is 'Lanoe' Captain Hawker VC, DSO, depicted in France in 1915. Lanoe Hawker (1890–1916) became one of Britain's first aces in mid-1915. Like his peers in the early days of the Royal Flying Corps, he had learnt to fly before the war. He was also a pioneering aviation engineer, credited with developing a forward-firing Lewis Gun on the Bristol Scout – as well as coming up with the idea of the warm aviator footwear known as 'fug boots'. It's appropriate, then, that these are depicted on this tiny figure of Lanoe.

This project was painted as a gift for Francisco Guedes to go with his DH2 model, and to acknowledge his facilitation of the Facebook Wingnut Wings Group. It is a faithful 1:32-scale representation of the young English ace, produced in white resin as part of a special-release aircraft kit by this now defunct but legendary World War I aircraft modelling company.

Mike Good, the talented US master, sculpted Lanoe. It has become one of the most sought-after figures from his Wingnut portfolio, after fellow New Zealand figure artist John Belcher shared his version. Mike kindly shared his expert critique on the initial stages of the painting, plus additional background. This included a wonderful photo of Lanoe, aged twenty-four, showing the ravages of only a few months in combat flying. Sadly he would be dead by the age of twenty-five, becoming the ill-fated eleventh victim of The Red Baron.

This project was a chance to trial a new 'Flesh' paint set from ScaleColours for Lanoe's face and hair. These tube acrylics have similar properties to bottle and jar acrylic formulations, but they don't suffer from pigment settling out, making them more user-friendly.

This palette was a worthwhile learning challenge, with primarily the ScaleColour six-tube set being one of the smallest palettes ever used for flesh painting. In addition it only needed Prussian Blue, used in minute amounts, a little for the eyes and iris, and Crimson for the lips. In this set Moss Green is used as a cooling tone, blended with Crimson and/or Burnt Skin for shadow tones, both mid and dark shadows. Each of the face areas is treated separately, with base, shadow and highlights being added and then blended into the surrounding area.

Lanoe's flesh and uniform were painted in acrylics, his other clothing in oils. Primer is not necessarily required on resin figures, however undercoating with complementary colours will help with the tones of the overcoat layers. For example, use a deep yellow for leather as it is beautifully bright and safe to use. One catch with this is that yellow is very transparent, so it needs a couple of coats or a white base coat. Without this, uneven coats result in dark patches of undercoat. However, this can be an advantage for weathering or shadow areas. Other underpainting colours for leather effects on oils include Turners Yellow,

Laying out a flesh palette to test a ScaleColour Artist acrylics set; all that was needed to fully balance this for Lanoe was to add a blue tone.

Vallejo Orange Brown and MSP Burnt Orange; all aim at adding light for a more translucent leather surface. These colours can be revealed by removing more oil paint so they show as highlights for well-worn leather.

A feature of this figure is the fur coat. Here the aim is to have a solid colour, with deep shadows and softer highlights. Looking at animal coats in life and in photographs will give a feel for how the fur or hair appears.

Overall this is a pleasing project that shows how different textures and surface effects can be achieved with different paint types.

Light and Pink Flesh from the ScaleColour set add warmness to the face; they were laid in from the forehead downwards to the neck.

Flesh painting was done directly on to the white resin base, with 'Burnt Skin' used for dark shadowing over a base flesh tone.

Minor adjustments, such as thin lips, were made to Lanoe's face after Mike Good reviewed 'in progress' photos.

Lights, camera, action! The working layout includes a water tray, wet palette, fine pointed brushes, acrylics, and tools to remove lint from the figure.

Painting Lanoe Hawker

Important Steps	Key Points (All paints Jo Sonja unless otherwise stated)
1. Paint flesh	* Painting the face loosely follows the following sequence: eyes, brow, nose, mouth, cheeks, chin, neck, ears and hair. * All the brushstrokes on the face tend to be done with a fine-pointed sable brush – #1 to block in colour, then fine detail with #00 or #10 × 0. * Flesh colours were blended with a mix of Vallejo Satin Varnish and Glaze Medium on the wet palette. * An extra dash of Satin Varnish was added to areas needing a little extra sheen – the brow, the upper part of the chin, the tip and bridge of the nose.
2. Paint cap and jacket	* Black is used as a base coat on the harsh white resin. Main jacket: *Base*: Green Oxide + Raw Sienna *Shadows*: Add Raw Umber to the base *Highlights*: Add Naples Yellow to the base * The technique used is mostly stibbling for the jacket, also an effort is made to darken the lower sleeve and jacket. At the first attempt we work around the figure, then down, rather than in sections.
3. Paint leather	* The leather belt and boots are undercoated with Citadel Golden Yellow. * The gloves and fur coat lining are undercoated with MSP Burnt Orange, then finished with Archival Mars Violet, Raw Sienna Dark. * The Sam Browne belt is polished leather: Archival Mars Violet, W&N Burnt Sienna. * The fug boots have a dense, dark, satin tone with flat reinforcing straps, toe and heel parts: *Main parts in oils*: W&N Burnt Umber, Yellow Ochre, Raw Sienna *Buff leather detail*: This is done with acrylic: Vallejo Panzer Aces Light Mud, with shading from Raw Sienna + Raw Umber, and finished using Naples Yellow highlights

(Continued)

Continued

Important Steps	Key Points (All paints Jo Sonja unless otherwise stated)
4. Paint the goatskin coat	* The fur coat is given a three-tone undercoat using Carbon Black, Raw Umber and Provincial Beige. * It is painted by stabbing and dabbing raw, dry oils fresh off a business card using an old '0'-tip brush with slightly splayed bristles. * The fur colours were built up with Archival Oils Raw Sienna Dark, W&N Naples Yellow, Titanium White and Rowney Sepia.
5. Paint the final details	*RFC Wings*: Base Raw Sienna, detail highlighted with Naples Yellow + Warm White *Captain pips*: Raw Sienna + Naples Yellow; shadow – Raw Umber Medal ribbons: *VC*: ScaleColour Red + Prussian Blue; *highlight* – ScaleColour Pink Flesh *DSO*: as VC above but redder, so a brighter, central band was painted first, then an outer band of Prussian Blue + Flesh to lighten the top edge

Matt Black was painted in hard-to-reach or deep shadow areas, plus as a base for the khaki green uniform.

Gloves, Sam Browne and boots use a Golden Yellow acrylic base to help create a glow for highlights beneath the oil paint.

Lanoe pioneered the use of fug boots, a signature dress item for him. An IWM photo painting reference shows that the leather is a rich chestnut brown.

Lanoe's coat is covered with thickened oils over the acrylic base, the aim being to get a multi-coloured, scrappy goatskin rather than softer fur.

The coat was painted with oils to give a softer effect to the fur. Note that the fabric coat lining on the jacket is also textured with acrylics.

An amazing likeness and personality was captured in Mike Good's sculpt. The final look tries to evoke the mood of a tired pilot, resigned to his fate.

Historical Note: William Rhodes-Moorhouse

The first pilot awarded the Victoria Cross (VC) had New Zealand Māori ancestors. He got the award for his actions on the day after the ANZAC landings at Gallipoli. Second Lieutenant William Rhodes-Moorhouse was the grandson of Ōtahui of Ngāti Ruanui and William Rhodes, a wealthy English whaling captain who settled in Wellington, New Zealand in the early nineteenth century. His VC was as a result of a successful, solo, low-level bombing raid he completed on the railway junction near Courtrai. His actions, described at the time in the *Waikato Times* as 'An Airman's Heroism – Gave His Life, But Saved His Machine' reflects yet another ambitious young flier, a pioneering aviator living a reckless life of flying and speed. He died the next day, 27 April 1915, aged twenty-seven, from a mortal thigh wound inflicted during the raid.

SOURCE: PAPERS PAST

Another 1/32 RFC pilot, sculpted by Benoit Cauchies, dressed in khaki and leather with an old-school Trinity College scarf, all painted in acrylics.

Pilots offer many options in dress and colour. This is Steve Warrilow's young Naval Air Service pilot with crew mate in an Oxford Blues scarf.

A favourite pair from Copper State Models both use thick acrylic paint – teased out for wool and ribbing on the scarf, plus MSP's leather mixes.

Converting and Painting Tommy's War Figure Kits

The figures for this project are Harry, Bob, Uncle and Jimmy, soldiers in the British Infantry 1917–18.

Author's Note

In many of our shared projects, Andy Belsey and I like to ring the changes with our Tommy's War figures by swapping out heads, hands and equipment. Darren Parker-Mead, the man behind Tommy's War, has also helped with supplying some extra heads, plus spare accessories in his kits. All the figures presented here, in the earlier Gallipoli hut section, and Percy below, are variations on the original figures supplied by Darren. In this feature section we focus on converting and painting these from the original figure kits.

Andy has converted Harry by adjusting his arms and adding new hands, plus a replacement Hornet head: this turns him into a unique-looking figure.

More additions can be seen, such as white epoxy filling gaps, a copper wire lanyard and D-ring, and white glue-soaked tissue for the helmet cover.

The Importance of Pose

With more than 100 World War I figures in this range, covering almost all combatants, Tommy's War is a versatile base for converting and personalizing. In conversions, begin by considering the subject, and most importantly the pose, then check the scale fit of the donor kits and parts. Nino Pizzichemi, the main sculptor of the range, does include natural variation in his figures, and as a result not all figures are necessarily suitable for a direct swap.

Also, when adding parts from other sculptors and manufacturers, further variety will be seen – for example, even though all items may be noted as 1:32 or 54mm, they can vary upwards to 1:30 (~60mm) or larger. Likewise with 1:35 (~50mm) items, these will also vary in size and bulk relative to each other. While precise measures can be taken, the best option is always to assess it by eye – if it looks wrong, it probably is, so try something else. Share conversions with others to get their impression and feedback too.

When deciding on the pose, study real photographs and also other modellers' work. The true master of figure posing is Bill Horan. Although not a World War I modeller, Bill's work cannot be beaten in terms of faith to the subject, originality and trademark presentation. Every one of his projects shows deliberate design in drama, storytelling and composition, from an individual figure to a three-figure vignette and multi-figure dioramas of many soldiers in action. His consistency over the years has inspired many to have a go at conversions, and his art is always a great starting point for getting a feel for how figures interact together.

Tip

Study the pose of a conversion, and painting stages, in a mirror to give an alternative perspective. This helps you to see what others would see, plus it is helpful in identifying anatomical errors and painting corrections.

The Rules of Proportions

When converting figures, especially if it means cutting into arm and leg joints, always keep in mind the basic rules of proportions. In particular be aware of the relationship between the head and the body parts, and the accessories and equipment. Normally figures are scaled by measuring their height from their feet to their eye level, although all sculptors have their own style and approach to scaling. Some tend to make their sculpts smaller, while others prefer bigger, each in an attempt to represent the natural variability of people in size and shape.

Consider also how to reinforce this variety by making sure to match weapons and personal kit with other figures featured in the same scene. Proportions of bodies may vary, but equipment should remain the same. Heads and hands also vary, so use a scale chart to help check your conversion. As a general rule for conversions consider the following rules:

* Figures are approximately 7½ to 8 heads tall
* The length of the hands is the same size as the face
* The length of the feet is the size of the head
* The length of the arms, with fingers extended, measures 3½ heads long, or reaches to about mid-thigh
* *See* plate later for more information

A Simple Conversion

One of the simplest conversions that all figure modellers can try is to exchange the kit head with another. For World War I modellers there are many options, beginning with the sculptor who set the standard for miniature heads – Roger Saunders. He produces heads in his ubiquitous Hornet range, and in the past for Verlinden Products. Other useful head options are from JSM, ModelCellar and Figurinitaly, and older ranges such as Scalelink, Historex and Airfix Multipose are still viable to customise Tommy's War and improve 1:35 plastic kitset figures.

When replacing a head, do give a thought to the expression and look on the face. Make sure this matches the pose and story the figure is conveying – for example, smiling works well for a restful scene, whereas animated faces or anxious looks are best for action scenes. Andy Belsey chose different heads for the first of the projects featured in this section, and he also adjusted the other kit heads. All have been painted as individual characters to illustrate the situation each soldier finds himself in.

Harry and Bob

'Harry' represents Harry Patch (1898–2009), who enlisted as Henry John Patch and became the last surviving British serviceman. He and friend 'Bob' were in the Duke of Cornwall's Light Infantry, and served together in the trenches at Passchendaele in 1917. It was with this in mind that Andy Belsey chose to depict his 'Reverse Trench' box display. Both prepare to repel a counterattack, having just occupied a German trench. Bob vigilantly surveys the terrain through his personal periscope, while

Harry waits pensively for the signal to return fire with his Lewis gun.

Harry has been converted to show the load bearing required for holding his Lewis gun. It set the benchmark for the squad automatic, becoming the most used light machine gun. It saw action with the Allies, including all British and Commonwealth units, US, Russian, Belgian (called the 'Rattlesnake') and Portuguese, as well as being sought after by German units.

The eyes have been positioned, the helmet painted black underneath to show tonal variation when painting flesh, and the gas-mask hose, made from guitar string, is filled with thick superglue.

Harry was only a teenager in World War I, so care was taken to depict his flesh tone as pinker and softer, to suit a more youthful complexion.

We experimented with new flesh tones to shape Harry's face by steadily working through different shading and highlights. Note the bloodshot right eye, too.

Weathering Figures in Muddy Terrain

Both Harry and Bob have the same colours for mud deliberately applied. Lighter colours indicate that the mud is drying, while lower sections are darkened to indicate wet or fresh mud. Note also that the pattern of splashes or smears differs because of the path chosen by each one to get to where they are. Machine gunners tend to spend a lot of time lying down because the gun is heavy, and needs to be supported on the ground to sight correctly. Normally gunners try to find higher ground to be able to cover the field ahead and provide more effective fields of fire – but high ground is not somewhere to stand, as the best sniper target is the silhouetted shape of an enemy.

There are useful mud patterns on this Tommy from lying down on his front, also splotches on the inside of his right shoulder from the butt of his weapon.
ROBIN BUCKLAND

A useful view of muddy detail on this sergeant resting in an infantry shelter; note the cover clipped over the working parts and fixed bayonet of his .303 SMLE.
ANDY BELSEY

TIP

Create a helmet cover and loose clothing with soft tissue soaked in PVA white glue mixed with water. As the glue dries it will stretch the tissue and create natural creasing.

Painting Harry

Important Steps	Key Points – Harry (All paints Jo Sonja unless otherwise stated)
1. Paint the eyes and flesh	*Undercoat*: Skintone Base *Shadows*: Burnt Sienna + Olive Green, Burnt Umber *Beard area*: Payne's Grey *Highlights*: Naples Yellow + VBeige Red *Cheeks and red tones*: Napthol Red Light *Lips*: VCad Umber Red *Lower*: + Naples Yellow for central highlight spot
2. Paint the jerkin	* Oils are used, as Lanoe's fug boots. * Use AK's Light Mud to depict the heavily muddied area, to show where Harry has lain in the mud.
3. Paint the base coat	* Carbon Black is prominent, though not used as a general undercoat, but rather for specific tasks: * to provide contrast to see faults * to fill deep shadow and undercut areas * for the base coat for Khaki Drab * Areas not requiring a dark base tone are not painted black – for example the helmet cover.
4. Paint the serge jacket	* Khaki uniform jacket and buff web gear use LifeColor (LC) World War I acrylics set from Italy. * Colours are different from the normal palette and work nicely when mixed with Jo Sonja. * Main base: LC Uniform Brown used with Burnt Umber shading and Naples Yellow highlighting. * Options: Consider less Uniform Brown or Olive Green when doing the trousers to show variety in the clothing material.
5. Paint the bags	*Base and shadow dirt*: Olive Green + Burnt Umber. *Ribbing pattern*: LC Webbing and Equipment 1 *Highlight*: VBuff stipple with a 5mm flat brush *Gas-mask haversack*: Green Oxide + Burnt Umber + Carbon Black painted in even layers using a soft pointed brush to show canvas effect.
6. Paint the helmet	*Inner rim*: Sap Green + Raw Umber *Cloth cover*: Raw Umber base with hessian texture stippled in horizontal and vertical lines using a flat 7mm brush. * Unit 'Battle Badge' is pencilled on the back of the cover with Carbon Black. * Note the ripped edge of the cover to expose the helmet rim.
7. Paint the trousers and puttees	*Base*: Carbon Black *Main*: LC Uniform Brown; *highlight*: Naples Yellow *Shadow*: Olive Green + Raw Umber + Carbon Black *Weathering*: AK Light Mud, Burnt Umber on the knees and front thigh from recently lying in position.
8. Paint the puttees	*Base*: LC Uniform Brown + Olive Green *Shadow*: Raw Umber *Highlights*: VBuff. Then washed with AK Light Mud + Burnt Umber from wading through the mire of the trenches.

(Continued)

Continued

Important Steps	Key Points – Harry (All paints Jo Sonja unless otherwise stated)
9. Paint the boots	*Base*: Burnt Umber, then washed as the puttees *Shadow*: Olive Green + Carbon Black **Note:** British boots were brown, and with dubbin waterproofing they became darker. Home issue boots for ceremonial purposes were black, and some of these would have turned up in the front line. Australian boots were also brown. Canadian and NZ soldier boots were black leather.
10. Paint the badges	Shoulder formation badge: *Base*: Carbon Black; add four wedges in Warm White; Central Dot with Napthol Light Red + Naples Yellow Lewis gunner qualification badge: * The painted background is slightly darker than the uniform sleeve colour. * Using a reference, carefully pick out the stitching with a #1 pointed sable using LC Uniform Brown, highlighted with Naples Yellow.
11. Paint the Lewis gun and pistol	*Base*: Carbon Black *Metals*: CLeadbelcher Oiled Steel *Blackened*: CAbaddon Black and CScorched Brown *Barrel Jacket*: Metals covered first with JSAll Purpose Sealer, then AK Worn Effects. Overpainted with VGame Colour Khaki. Remoistened with water, and the paint chipped and scratched with the toothpick *Woodwork*: VSaddle Brown + VNew Wood

Oil paint is laid out on business cards to remove excess oils and help reduce final sheen.

Harry looks serene in resin, however once paint is applied he starts to look like a determined young man ready to go.

Oils were used for the leather on Harry, as their gentle sheen gives an authentic effect, especially for larger leather surfaces.

Another way to convey character is by depicting Harry wearing a baggy jacket, as compared to the tailored clothing of Bob and Uncle.

Choose a bright undercoat for leather, which gives depth when it is covered with oil paint. An alternative is light green.

A sorry-looking wet palette at the completion of Harry, after much acrylic mixing. Paints are added around the outside, and mediums put in the centre section.

Photo set-up with key settings: 1. ISO100 for light sensitivity. 2. Shutter speed 6in. 3. Aperture 16. 4. Auto White Balance. The result can be seen in the next photo.

The weathering on the figure followed the photo references: mud-encrusted lower sleeves from resting with the Lewis gun, and on the backside and legs from sliding down into the trench.

It is risky blowing up figures for close study as my 'style' is far from clean. However, it is invaluable as a way to see faults for correction.

What Harry lacks in colour variation he makes up for in textures. Each is a painting experiment to replicate man-made surfaces.

TIP

Leave painting metal surfaces until last as these can be quite fiddly. Also use a separate palette with dedicated brushes to avoid contaminating other colours with tiny bits of metallic pigment.

Captain Bob's Uniform and Periscope

Bob is completed as a captain in the 7th Service Battalion of the Duke of Cornwall's Light Infantry, part of the 61st Brigade, 20th Infantry Division. He is armed with a Smith and Wesson .455 pistol. His grimy appearance is consistent with having to run across No Man's Land and scurry down into the enemy lines during the battle.

Notable in this depiction of a British officer in the trenches of 1916–18 is the personal pocket periscope made by Lifeguard. Andy has painstakingly crafted this. It is a tiny model in its own right, using white plastic strip and reflective film for the mirror, plus a tinfoil badge. It took three hours to paint, including the addition of dots of bronze paint to show the many hinge bolts on the expandable lattice.

The conversion changes that are visible: added helmet, liner and strap, respirator bag, lanyard cord, new left hand with cuff rank, brass pistol barrel, and the moustache has been removed.

All flesh base coated and the eyes detailed. Although the helmet liner and open mouth look stark painted in black, the later stages will tone these down.

The face is steadily improving with a systematic approach working from the top down and on specific areas around the eyes, nose, mouth, cheek and ears.

The Brodie helmet has been roughly daubed with an early version Apple Green colour. Also shown is the harness arrangement for securing the gas-mask haversack.

Painting Bob

Important Steps	Key Points – Bob (All paints Jo Sonja unless otherwise stated)
1. Paint the face and skin	Eyes: *Base*: VLight Flesh *Upper lash and eye*: Carbon Black *Iris*: Payne Grey, Highlight: Naples Yellow *Corners*: Thin wash VCadmium Umber Red Face: *Base*: Skintone Base *Shadows*: Burnt Sienna + Sap Green *Beard* (known as 5 o'clock shadow): Burnt Umber + Brilliant Magenta *Highlights*: Naples Yellow + VBeige Red *Cheeks, lips and red tones*: Napthol Red Light + VCad Umber, Highlight: Naples Yellow Mouth: *Tongue*: VBeige Red *Teeth*: Warm White *Saliva*: Gloss varnish was used to show saliva on both Fingers: Face flesh colour with nails added with VLight Flesh and a coating of satin varnish.
2. Paint the helmet	*Base*: Green Oxide with satin varnish *Shadow*: Raw Umber *Weathered*: Grit and mud wash from crushed Faber Castell Tan pastel and Brown Earth.

(Continued)

Continued

Important Steps	Key Points – Bob (All paints Jo Sonja unless otherwise stated)
	Alternative colour option from Tony Barton, 1:6 World War I figure maestro: * Early issue 1916 Brodies were a dull apple green; this colour was replaced by khaki by 1917. * Try V823 Luftwaffe Camouflage Green for the former and V70873 US Field Drab for the latter. * Later helmets usually had sand mixed into the paint to creating a rough matt finish.
3. Paint the uniform	*Shirt Collar*: Fawn + Raw Sienna Jacket: *Base*: Carbon Black, then Main: Olive Green *Shadow*: Raw Umber *Highlight*: Naples Yellow *'Battle badge'*: The unit battle badge is stitched on the upper back in black cloth and thread; this is done with built-up layers of Carbon Black Trousers: *Outer – base*: LifeColor Uniform Green; *shade*: Raw Umber, Carbon Black; *highlight*: Fawn, Naples Yellow *Inner – base*: Fawn; *shade*: Raw Umber; *highlight*: Naples Yellow
4. Paint the gas-mask haversack	As Harry
5. Paint the boots	*Base*: Fawn; *shade*: CRinox Hide *Highlight*: Liquitex Heavy Body Acrylic Raw Sienna – this is an excellent paint to work with, slightly thicker, creamy like soft butter and with a slight but pleasing sheen *Weathering*: AK Dry Light Mud, Burnt Umber
6. Paint the leather equipment	*Satchel black leather – base*: Raw Sienna; *shadow*: Raw Umber + Carbon Black + Satin Varnish; *highlight*: Raw Sienna + Olive Green *Satchel upper – base*: Naples Yellow; *shadows*: Raw Umber; *highlights*: Warm White *Sam Browne, holster and Lifeguard pouch – base*: LCRed Leather; *shade*: LCDark Leather, Burnt Umber, Carbon Black; *highlight*: Raw Sienna
7. Paint the metal equipment	As Harry's weapon without overpainting Periscope: *Inner bars*: Nimbus Grey *Outer bars*: VLight Grey *Shadow*: Raw Umber *Top and Bottom*: VSatin Black *Bolt heads*: Carbon Black spot with Golden Fluid Iridescent Bronze

There is lots of colour in this lieutenant's uniform and equipment, which was common, as officers supplemented service issue with tailored and privately purchased items. ROBIN BUCKLAND

Flesh effects include flushed cheeks, beard shadow, tiny fingernails and dirty hands. These flesh tones can be gauged against the weathered helmet and tan collar.

Choosing base colours is crucial. The jacket colour is textured over a black base, with light tan for dark leather, and the green helmet has a roughened dirt finish.

The holster, belt and boots show use of a lighter-tone base with the darker leather washes to give both sheen and depth to these items.

The figure is securely held against the workbench for finishing the metal parts, shoulder badge and cuff rank, as each requires a steady hand and precision painting.

The scaled-down Lifeguard periscope has two small squares of film for mirrors, which reflect the up and down intricate lattice extension.

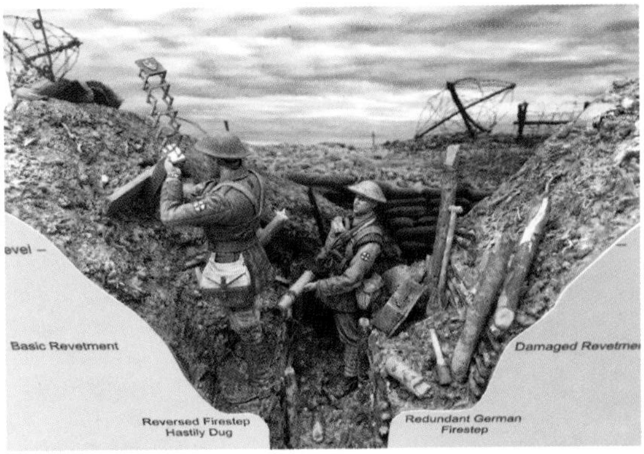

In Andy's 'Reversed Trench' Bob stands part way up a slope, looking over the German trench parados, shouting 'Steady lads!' down to Harry and his pals.
ANDY BELSEY

Tip

Priming resin is generally unnecessary, instead do undercoat deliberately as a base coat and build other colour layers over it.

The primed figure from Andy, with a new forefinger made from plastic rod, a replacement helmet and a foil helmet strap. Both arms were adjusted to hold a map.

Uncle and Jimmy, Subalterns

The East Surreys shaped the popular folklore of British World War 1 experience in two ways. One was the famous 'Footballers' chase' by the 8th Battalion in July 1916. The second was through *Journey's End*, a contemporary play by R.C. Sherriff, a young veteran of the post-Somme Ypres offensive.

Uncle and Jimmy are subalterns from the East Surrey Regiment who fought in Arras, 1917–18. These figures were simpler conversions by Andy, built to appear in his underground dugout scene. Both had arms rearranged, and heads adjusted to tell the story of a pair of officers taking time out from night raids. The painting of the figures was inspired by the 2017 film adaption of Sherriff's play, especially the standing officer. Here, effort was made to get a uniform with a heavily weathered and chalky effect, consistent with his time in this area of the line, as shown in the movie, in which he is played by British actor Paul Bettany.

A minor addition to Andy's figure was a pair of tiny spectacles worn by the character. These were made with five pieces of thin brass rod, each piece cut with modelling snips, twisted with a small pair of pliers and then superglued together. Elmer's Clear Glue was used to fill the glass lens, and when dry this was coated with gloss varnish. The glasses were not painted, but instead were left to dull naturally over time.

Jimmy was an easier prospect for painting. His exposed, snoring face peering out from under the grey army blanket, with its stitched red border, would still be an interesting feature when tucked away into the back of the bunker.

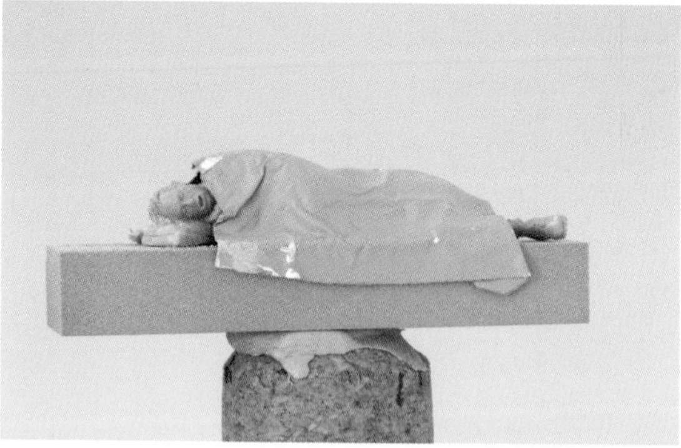

Jimmy, on a temporary softwood block, dozes under a foil dish blanket; both are primed with the grey spray primer paint that Andy prefers.

Tip

Never use the same flesh colours on different projects, but instead vary the mixes on the palette – a little less here, and more there, to experiment with capturing the complexion of each new figure.

Painting Hands – As Important as Faces

Hands and faces are one of the most important considerations for figures. They each add humanity to a person and deserve special attention. If these are not correct, do reshape, refine or replace them. Spare hand sets are available from Hornet, Royal, Historex and Figurinitaly. Alternatively they can be built by drilling out the hand, adding thin brass wire, then covering and shaping detail from putty.

Paint hands directly after the face is done using the same palette in the following sequence:

1. Block in the overall flesh colour using the first shadow colour of the face palette.
2. Work on the back of the hand, comparing it with the back of your own hand, adding veins with a little blue or green, then highlights for tendons, and continue to build up the effect without overdoing any element. Judge the effect of the finished hands once the surrounding areas are completed.
3. The focus of the fingers is first on the shadows and then the warm red areas around the joints, then highlights for the fleshy sections.
4. Finally do the fingernails. Initially add a mid-shadow base for the shape, then highlight with a light pinkish white, the same tone as the white of the eyes. Last is a touch of extra satin varnish to give lustre.

Once the eyes were finished, it was time to test the tiny brass spectacles' frame on the bridge of Uncle's nose to check how to paint the face around this 'obstacle'.

Uncle's helmet has thin streaks of weathering colours dragged down from the top to replicate rain washing off mud and chalk.

TIP

When painting a figure consider using related or complementary colours to maintain balance or harmony throughout the figure – for example Olive Green is suitable in flesh, clothing, equipment and weathering. Use a colour wheel as a guide for showing how colours complement and relate to each other.

TIP

Make the badges with built-up layers of unthinned Jo Sonja paint taken direct from the tube. Make sure that each layer is dry before adding the next.

Painting Uncle and Jimmy

Important Steps	Key Point: Uncle and Jimmy (All paints Jo Sonja unless otherwise stated)
1. Paint the flesh	As Harry and Bob
2. Paint the uniform	*Base*: Carbon Black AK World War I British Uniforms Set was the basis for Uncle's uniform. Jacket: *Base*: British Uniform Mid Tone + SapGreen/Carbon Black: *Shadow*: + British Uniform Shadow + Black *Highlight*: + Naples Yellow Trousers: As the jacket, but Mid Tone was replaced with Light Tone, and in the shadow Burnt Umber was used instead of Carbon Black. East Surrey shoulder badges were made with thick-layered acrylic paint: *Diamond* – base: Napthol Red Crimson with Raw Umber shadow *Rectangle* – base: Hookers Green, Base + Naples Yellow *Cuff rank ribbon*: Fawn painted in fine lines with a #1 sable brush **Note:** The left cuff title rank from Magic Sculpt was added as it had been missed off the original sculpt.
3. Paint leather	The LifeColor World War I Uniform set was the basis for the leather. Sam Brown and holster: *Base and highlight*: LC Red Leather *Shadow*: LC Dark Leather + Burnt Umber Black leather: *Base*: Fawn *Shadow*: VBlack + Hookers Green and Jo Sonja Satin Varnish *Highlight*: Skintone
4. Paint the boots	*Base and highlights*: VOrange Brown *Shadow*: Burnt Sienna + Burnt Umber

(*Continued*)

Continued

Important Steps	Key Point: Uncle and Jimmy (All paints Jo Sonja unless otherwise stated)
5. Paint the helmet	*Base*: Green Oxide with satin varnish *Shadow*: Burnt Umber and Burnt Sienna dabbed over the base *Highlight*: Base + Naples Yellow
6. Paint weathering	*Over the lower parts of the jacket, trousers and boots*: Washes of Light Mud + Warm White *Shadow*: Raw Umber
7. Paint the army blanket	*Base*: Payne's Grey; *shadow*: Black; *highlight*: Naples Yellow. All colours dabbed with a worn #2 brush *Red stitching*: Napthol Crimson

The jacket colour has lighter stippling on the upper surface, darker in the mid-back shadow, and darkest for the seams. Black is left for gaps, such as under the epaulettes and collar.

Badges, such as the red formation diamond, the dark green stripe below, and the service stripes on the right cuff, are all built up with thick layers of acrylic paint.

The right side view of Uncle has lots of colour and effects such as the undershirt woollen cuff, the chipped binoculars and the tarnished brass on the satchel.

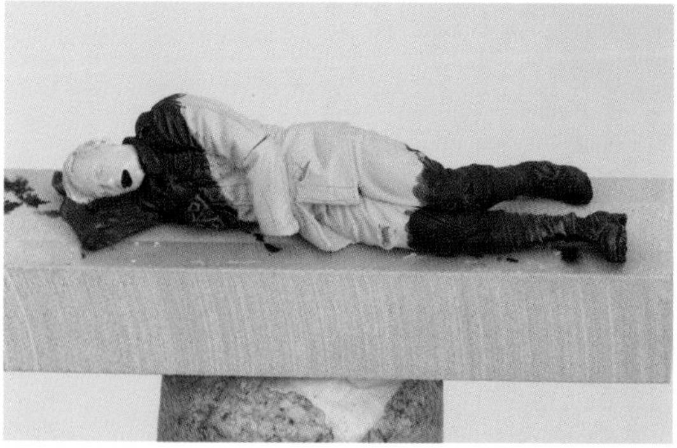

With the blanket removed the black base for painting khaki is revealed, and the wounded gunner figure that Andy changed to become a sleeping subaltern.

There is no need to paint the area covered by the blanket as it won't be seen. However, a great deal of attention was concentrated on getting a young, restful, snoring face.

The heavy, grey woollen blanket with its trademark red stitching was textured in the same way as a larger uniform area. Note the hand detail and the small finger separated out.

The binoculars' case has a darker leather finish to contrast with the Sam Browne and boots leather. Splashes of chalky mud were incorporated in the weathering.

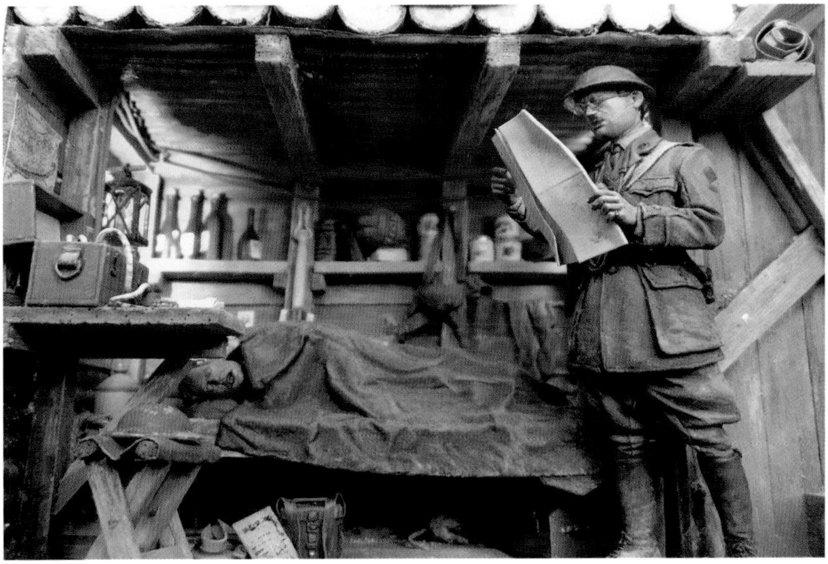

Andy placed both figures into an officer's bunker, below the trench line. His book has a full explanation of how this was created.

ANDY BELSEY

Historical Note

Were World War I British uniforms too bland and boring? Consider adding variety into scenes by showing them as, or with prisoners, such as a German Uhlan or an Austro-Hungarian Hussar. Or mix up the nations – for example the US Infantry first went into action on 4 July 1918, alongside Australian infantry in the Battle of Hamel. Despite many being pulled from the support reserves by General 'Blackjack' Pershing, four companies did stay to become part of the attack. Their clean, smart attitude and new uniforms were distinctive against the battle-weary veteran Aussies. Consider how you might show the different look of each, not just in uniform, but also in look and feel.

Percy, another Andy Belsey figure. New Zealand troops were issued with khaki shirts. Fine painting effects were used on the face, uniform and bare arms.

Chapter Six

Resin and Metal Busts

PAINTING A WHITE METAL BUST

This work-in-progress 1:16 white metal bust of the poilu 'François' is used to explain working with metal figures and using oils for texturing, especially hair and fur.

Preparing the Bust

Most busts are bigger than figures, usually 1:10 (180mm) to 1:6 (300mm); however, there is a

Author's Note

With my ancestors from Normandy and France, modelling military forces from this nation is a natural choice, and an important World War I subject when combined with the unbelievable sacrifice France made in World War I, best typified by the horrific battle of Verdun.

Poilus of the 219th Infantry Regiment move forwards to relieve another unit c.1916. All are heavily clothed and rugged up for the cold conditions. OLIVÈRES COLLECTION

TIP

Always use enamel Matt Black or Matt White as a primer to seal metal and as a base surface for painting. In older figures this can also help protect against lead rot or oxidation of the metal.

growing group of smaller busts based around 1:16 (120mm) figures. This one from Metal Modeles is such a bust. Despite being smaller, there is still plenty of potential to convey personality, even in the reduced form. This bust will be a homage to the ancestors of a young modelling friend, Yannick Olivères, who is part of a new generation of modellers who are choosing military subjects over fantasy ones. Yannick's family has a proud military history, as his grandfather François Louis Noël Olivères (24ème Régiment d'Infanterie) and his great uncle François Marie Célis Collin (99ème Régiment d'Infanterie) both served as poilus in the French army. The 24th spent time in Verdun, so this will be the choice for the collar tab on this bust.

This Metal Modeles bust is sold as Légion Étrangère, Fusilier France 1918. As a French Foreign Légionnaire (FFL) François would have had a khaki mustard uniform, not Bleu Horizon as worn by the poilu.

In the following table are the steps necessary for preparing this bust for painting, plus a colour palette recommended by Yannick.

Young French poilus of the 24th Infantry at Louviers, 5 September 1915. Note their mix of clothing items and different uniform colours. OLIVÈRES COLLECTION

The original bust (L) compared to the ready-to-paint version (R), with unnecessary detail filled – the Foreign Legion badge and the sculpted iris of the right eye.

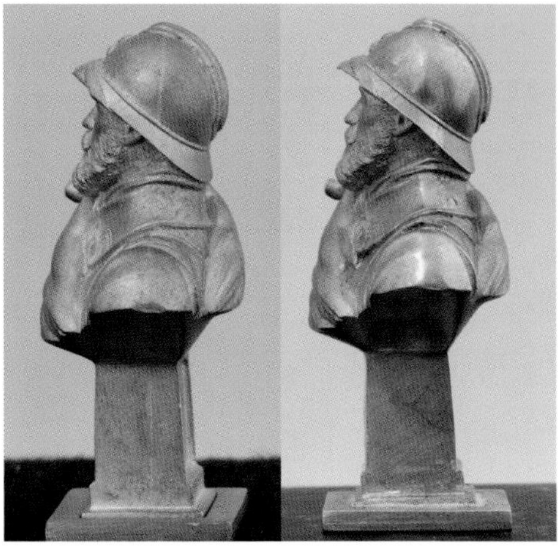

White metal casting uses a two-part mould, normally leaving a fine cast line (L), easily polished off (R) by filing and with fine sandpaper.

Preparing the Bust for Painting

Important Steps	Key Points
1. Remove the fine mould line	* Use a sharp blade to carefully shave off the mould line. * Smooth the shaved areas with superfine-grade sandpaper.
2. Fill any unnecessary detail	* Fill any awkward mould line detail or flaws left from the first step above. Use epoxy putty to fill the pupils of the scalloped eyes. * Use putty to fill the FFL badge on the base, and smooth the putty with handcream, after curing the sand putty surface to ensure it is blended into the base. * Fill the collar tab number '1' and replace it with the painted '24', which represents Yannick's grandfather's unit.
3. Add the bandage over the eye	* Make the wound dressing with bunched-up plumber's thread tape. * Use thread tape for the bandage. * Secure the bandage in place with small spots of CA superglue – be careful not to use too much of this as it will damage the thin thread tape.
4. Prime the metal	* Spray the prepared bust using a can of Citadel Chaos Black. * Warm the can in hot water, then shake it vigorously before use. * Spraying is done in a series of quick strokes, beginning off the bust, moving in a smooth motion across it, and finishing off it on the other side. This avoids large droplets landing on the bust itself.
5. Apply a thick coat of oil to the hair area	* Winsor and Newton Naples Yellow is applied with a large flat brush. * Use the paint directly from the tube. Do not add thinner when laying paint on to the bust, as this prevents it building up.

(Continued)

Continued

Important Steps	Key Points
6. Work the hair detail into the oil paint	* Leave the paint to cure for approximately 20–30 minutes. * Use a fine pointed tool such as a dental instrument, darning needle, pin or sharpened toothpick to simulate hair. * As the paint dries, further finer hair can be teased out. * Keep working the surface until the paint becomes too stiff to tease. * Leave to dry, at least overnight.
7. Paint the hair (still to be done)	* Hair can be painted once dry with thin oil washes or acrylics. * If using acrylics consider a satin finish brand such as Matisse or Vallejo.
8. Paint the bust (still to be done)	Yannick Olivères Bleu Horizon colour palette: 1915 Bleu Horizon (All Vallejo): *Base*: Black Grey + French Mirage Blue + a hint of Luftwaffe Blue + Grey Blue *Highlights*: Sky Blue + Mirage Blue *Shadows*: Black Grey + French Mirage Blue Helmet Semi-Gloss Blue: (All Vallejo) *Base*: Prussian Blue + Grey Blue + French Mirage Blue *Highlights*: Grey Blue + French Mirage Blue *Shading*: Glossy Black + Black Grey + a hint of Grey Blue *Final coat*: Well thinned glaze of Black Grey to tone down the blue *See more* on painting Bleu Horizon in 'Finished Figure Projects'.

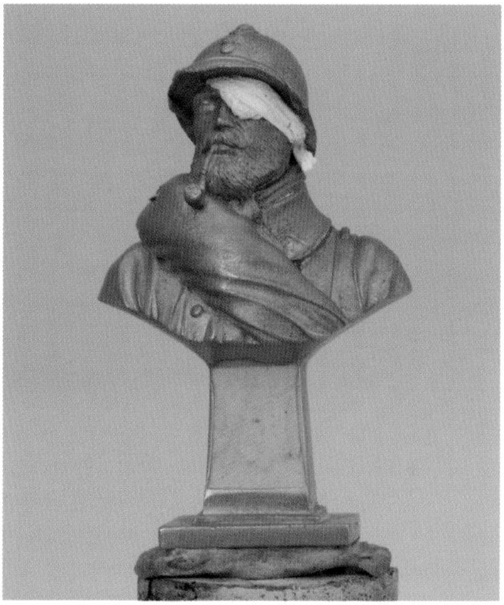

The heavily bandaged eye adds a personal touch; it includes a folded pad over the eye and a bandage tassel at the back.

The bust secured to the dowel for painting, firstly with an enamel black primer spray. Plumber thread tape was used to create the bandage.

The eye was started with Light Flesh undercoat (L), then attention was focused on the position and shape of the iris (R), before detailing with acrylics.

Facial hair was built up with thick W&N Naples Yellow, then teased out with a sharpened toothpick point and a darning needle.

CONVERTING A RESIN BUST

Gas became a weapon during World War I, with all sides using it in an attempt to gain an advantage in the stalemate that was trench warfare. French forces were actually the first to use gas in 1914, albeit a non-lethal tear gas. It was the arrival of highly toxic, lethal chlorine gas, released in Ypres

The concept mockup, with the help of Yannick Olivères who recoloured the boxart to a Bleu Horizon poilu. The final look will depict weariness, filth and a bloodied dressing.

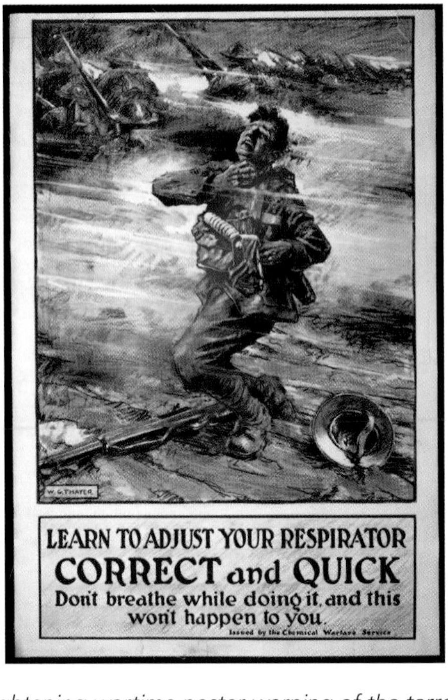

A frightening wartime poster warning of the terror and fear caused from gas attacks when a respirator is not used quickly. LIBRARY OF CONGRESS

against French troops early in 1915, that would change the face of the war for frontline soldiers. However, chlorine's disadvantages of being highly visible as a coloured gas, along with an easily detected smell, meant it was relatively short-lived. More deadly examples, such as phosgene, were soon developed, and tested on human targets in late 1915. Other gases would follow in an attempt to be a more silent and deadly prelude to attacks, or to disable enemy forces.

Reaching into a gas-mask bag for his PH hood, the main protection against gas in 1915 and early 1916; later the hood was carried as a backup to the gas mask. SOURCE: Reconstruction of British infantryman's uniforms courtesy of Mike Everest and Mike South of The 10th Essex Living History Group.

Simple defensive measures were quickly developed to provide some form of protection from gas. To begin with, wet or urine-soaked rags provided some relief from chlorine. Soon after, more sophisticated breathing and eye protection began to be developed. For the British this began with the P helmet and the PH hood, a chemically treated cloth hood easily dropped over the head. However, this proved ineffective against later gases, which led to the development of the 'small box respirator' (SBR). This would become standard use for all British, Commonwealth and American Expeditionary Forces (AEF) when they arrived in France in late 1916, early 1917.

Helmet clenched between his legs, he unfurls the soft flannel hood. These were coloured light to dark grey-blue.

Pulling on the gas mask – this was always uncomfortable, and even more so with the hood, which smelt, was claustrophobic, and could burn the skin if too wet.

For the mask to work properly it needed to be tucked down inside the jacket collar, and breathing was done through the red flutter valve.

The SBR took its name from the small canister that helped filter the gas-laden air. This was carried in a haversack, normally on the chest, though it could also be carried on the side, or over the top of the pack when moving to and from the line. This haversack contained the canister in one side pouch, and the gas mask itself in the other. A particular feature to note is that the haversack was normally worn backwards on the chest so the flap opened away from the body, meaning the mask could be grabbed more quickly in an emergency. The mask itself was a rubber-coated canvas material that was a lifesaver if put on quickly.

This project of 'Herb', a Lewis gunner, started out as a personal conversion of a World War I British soldier, produced by Young Bok Song. His brand, Young Miniatures, is a highly regarded South Korean company that has produced a range of hand-sculpted busts for over a decade. They are well known for the quality of casting, and careful attention paid to achieving a visually pleasing representation of a wide variety of subjects from across the ages.

Included in the range are a couple of World War I busts, one of which is a youthful-looking Lewis gunner. He has an open gas-mask bag on

SBR was introduced in 1916, with a stockinet-covered rubber breathing hose, filter box canister, and attached gas exposure card to record when the filter needed replacement. SOURCE: Reconstruction of SBR courtesy of Mike Everest of The 10th Essex Living History Group.

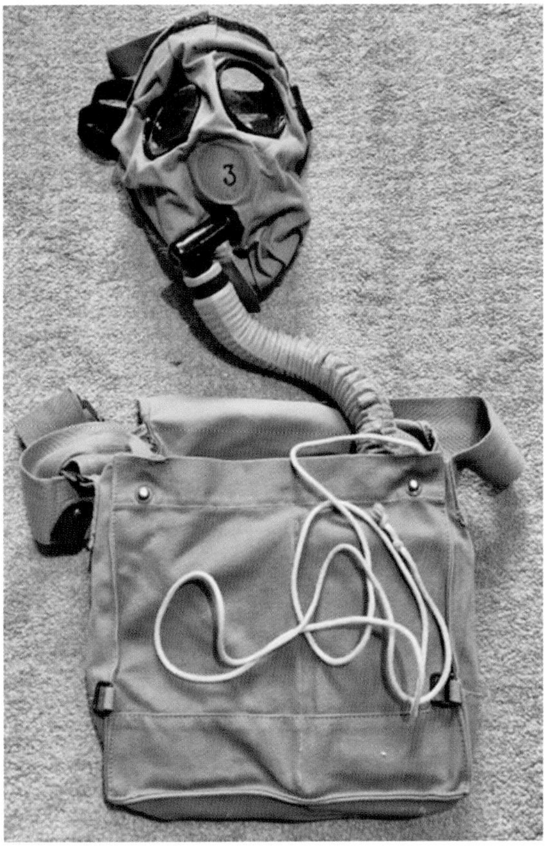

The Mk1 Haversack front – this side was secured against the chest with the waxed cord. Gas mask size '3' is stamped on the nose-clip circle.

his chest, and a recently used SBR gas mask hanging limply over the side of the bag. It was therefore ideal to reimagine him, instead with his gas mask in place on his face. Researching various photos and reference books uncovered more details that could be used to convert the bust into an authentic look for a British soldier in the thick of a gas attack.

After sharing this concept with Young he suggested that this could be a project that would be produced as a special limited edition for his range. It was decided to provide two head options, one with the mask over a bare head, and another with the helmet in position, each requiring the addition of the mask straps to keep it securely in place. Other changes made from Young's original sculpt were to turn the bag round to the reversed position, and to create an extension of the rubber hose.

It was also decided to move the hand away from covering the end of the barrel jacket, a practice that would incur the wrath of many a drill instructor who would scream at a young recruit that 'that is not the way to handle a weapon, laddie!' This also allowed for a cover to be added to the barrel. Each of these changes gives a distinctively different-looking bust, with a different attitude.

Note: The actual design of the final release of this Young's Special Edition bust differs slightly due to production constraints.

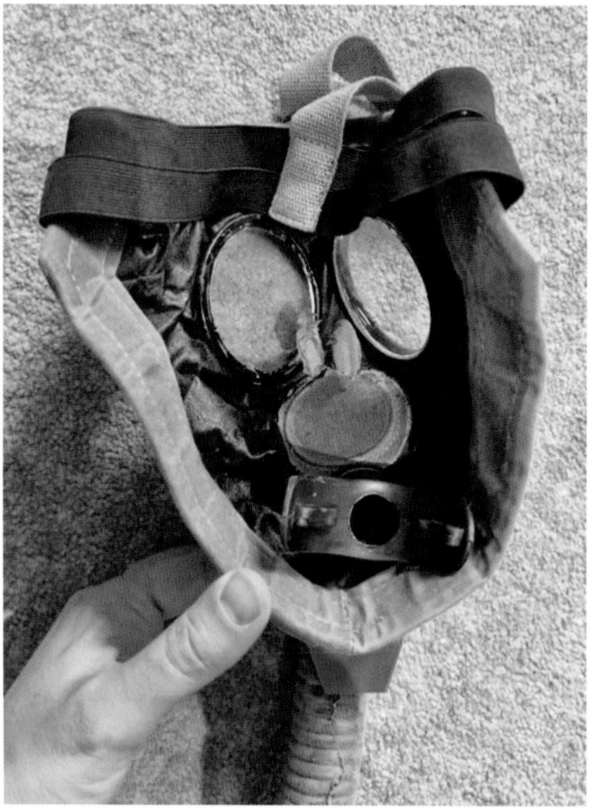

A useful inside view, for those with Young's original bust, shows the nose clip, breathing mouthpiece, rubber coating, black elastic and tan fibre bands.

Original production bust (L) magnificently painted by professional artist Kirill Kanaev, and the conversion (R) with the repositioned hand cradling the Lewis gun.

'Herb', a Lewis Gunner

Important Steps	Key Points
1. Remove unnecessary parts	* The chin strap on the face is not required, so it can be carefully filed and sanded off. * The flap from the back edge of the haversack is removed using a sharp, broad-bladed XActo knife. * The haversack tie-down rings were used to secure the bag to the chest to prevent it bouncing about when the wearer was running.
2. Refine the mask	* Thin out the back of the mask using a motor tool (also known as a Dremel tool), being careful not to break through the side of the resin. * Regularly test fit the parts. * Finish with fine-grade sandpaper.
3. Rebuild the haversack	* The inside of the haversack is hollowed out – the left side is empty. * Use putty on the right side to show the top of the canister. * Putty is used to reshape the front surface. * Add a new flap folded forwards from the front edge of the haversack. * Position the flap while the putty is soft, then shape it properly when the putty is dry. * Inside domes are added with circles, punched out of plastic card, and drilled hollow.
4. Rework the head	* Option 1 has a bareheaded section built up using epoxy putty, then the hair is carved with a fresh, sharp scalpel blade. Also, a smoothed strip was created down the line of the hair parting to take the fibre strap that stretches across the centre of the head. * Option 2 has a helmet with chinstrap and buckle added from putty, and shaped with a sharpened toothpick tool.
5. Rebuild the mask edging and add the straps	* Smear the face with a thin coating of Vaseline. * Add a new mask edging from putty, fit it to the face, and work wrinkles with a soft rubber brush. * Leave the putty to dry. Remove the mask and fine-tune the edging with a scalpel. * Clean the Vaseline from the face with hot soapy water and white spirit. * Once the face is dry, retest the fit of the mask, and correct deviations with fresh putty as needed. * Roll out thin strips of putty to make each side strap. Allow to partially cure. Lay out the straps one at a time, and smooth into position with a firm rubber brush. * Leave to dry, and then sharpen the strap detail with a scalpel to show the tension around the head.
6. Extend the breathing hose	* Drill a hole in the top of the canister and the hose fitting on the mask. * Use Blu Tack to attach the haversack and mask in position. * Push a length of copper wire or solder into the mask fitting, then curve and shape it into the hole in the canister top. * Remove the wire and build up the thickness using strips of putty, until the diameter of the hose is reached. Leave to dry. * Using a needle file and knife blade, remove thin rings of putty to fabricate the ribbed effect of the breathing hose.

(Continued)

Continued

Important Steps	Key Points
7. Refine the hand	* Use a scalpel to open up and separate the fingers. * Cut wedges out of the finger joints. * Using pliers to hold each finger while carefully warming the resin, gently straighten out each finger, then immerse the hand in cold water to lock the finger in its new position. * Fingernails were re-sculpted with a thin layer of putty and a toothpick.
8. Add the Lewis gun-barrel jacket cover	* Roll out two thin strips of putty. * Take one strip and wrap it round the barrel jacket. Add a seam using a flattened toothpick tip. * Cut a disc out of the other thin strip. Moisten the top edging of the barrel jacket strip with hand lotion, add the disc and make the seam line as each strip is blended together. * Create ties for the cover with offcuts from the putty strips.

Tip

* Use Vaseline to prevent wet epoxy putty sticking to another surface.
* To straighten or reposition a resin part, soften it in hot water or hot air blown from a hairdryer. Be careful not to overheat it, as this could damage detail on the part.

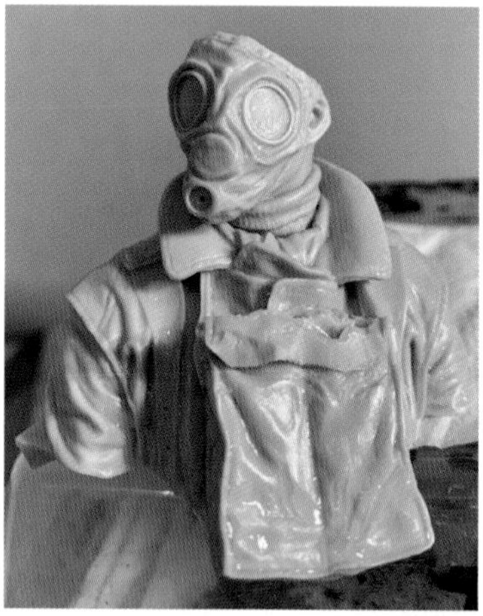

Test fitting the hollowed mask and opening up the top of the original kit haversack, worn here in the 'alert' position on the jerkin.

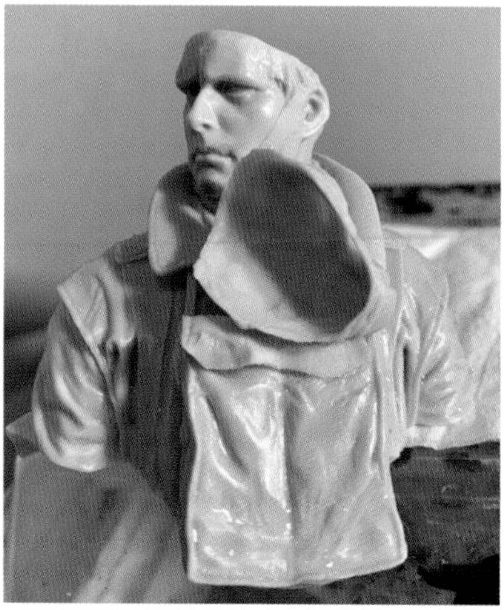

The bust conversion began by removing the chinstrap with the knife and sanding the cheeks smooth, then hollowing out the mask to fit flush on the face.

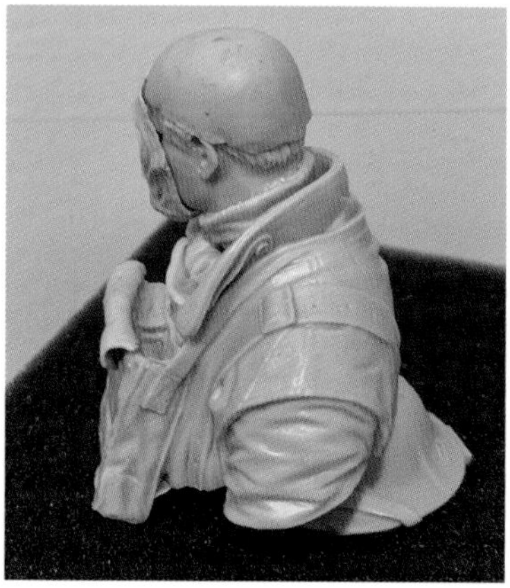

A blob of putty was shaped and smoothed with hand cream to form the bare head section.

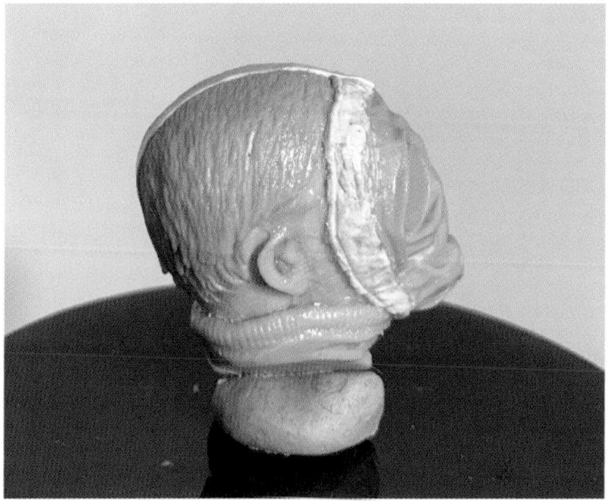

The face was coated with Vaseline, to prevent Apoxie putty sticking to the resin, as the mask edging was fitted snugly to the face.

The parts for the helmeted option with the corrugated breathing hose temporarily fitted to the mask front and into the top of the canister in the haversack.

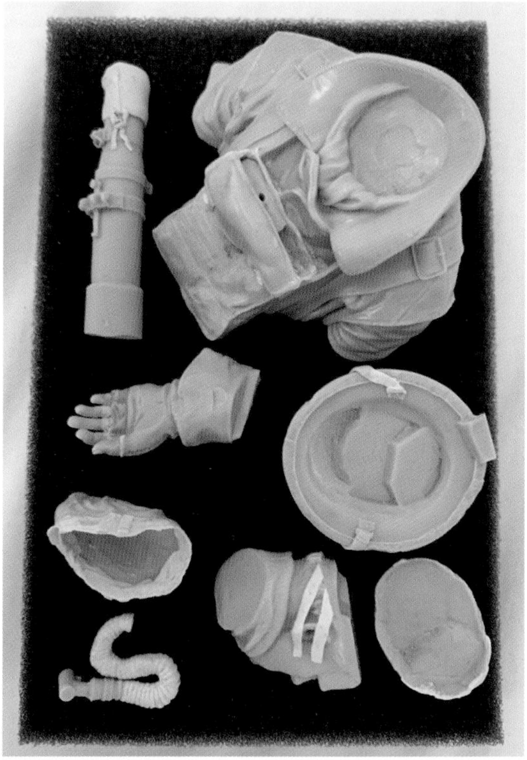

The parts breakdown as supplied to Young for further refinement prior to production as a Special Edition bust.

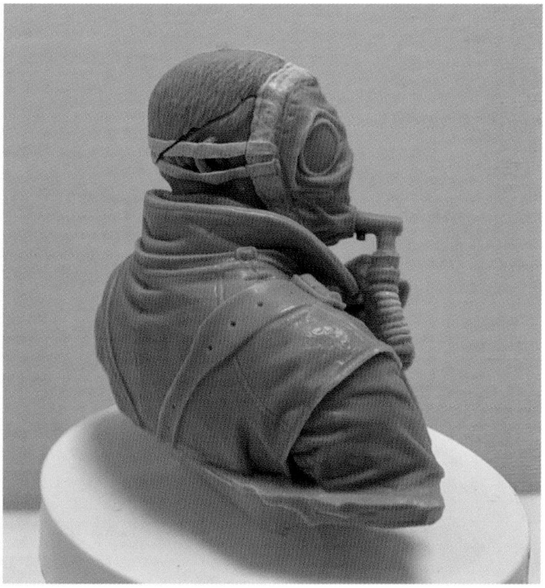

The right side view shows the bare head option, with the elastic harness straps and the outlet in the angle tube for fitting the flutter valve.

Chapter Seven

Painting Busts

Painting Eyes and Faces

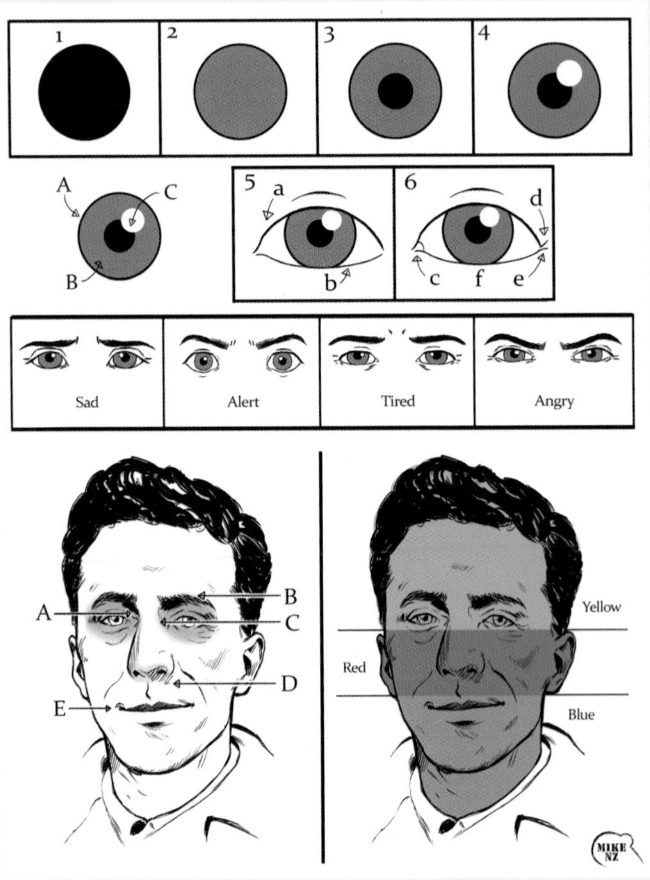

(Continued)

Continued

There are four steps to painting eyes in scales from 1:35–1:32 upwards. Larger scales allow more detailing, but follow the same basic approach.

Always begin with a light pinkish base colour, typically Vallejo Light Flesh, then follow the sequence of steps below:

1. Iris – use Carbon Black and focus on the position, shape and size.
2. Overlay with the iris colour (B), leaving the outer rim black (A).
3. Add the pupil – repeat until it is centrally placed.
4. Add the catchlight (C) – this can be pure white, or an extreme highlight of the iris colour. Catchlight indicates the direction of the light – so this is sun/light coming from the top left.
5. The eye shape is typically almond, with a slightly flatter (less curved) bottom lash. Lashes define the shape:
   * Use black for the upper lash – it always covers part of the eyeball.
   * Use dark brown for the lower lash – it may not cover the eyeball, so there may be a little eye white visible above the lash, for example when the eyes are alert or looking upwards.
6. Eye detailing:
   * Use Napthol Red Light thinned in the corners of the eye.
   * Make a crease up from the outside corner.
   * Make another crease out from the corner above the cheeks.
   * For larger figures: add a lighter upper section to the iris and shade the lower part of the sclera with Naples Yellow.
   * When complete, consider gloss varnishing the eyes to add natural reflection, especially on larger-scale figures and busts.

Expressions are mainly conveyed through the eyes and brow. Common examples here can be painted on smaller faces, or adjust features with putty on larger figures.

Surroundings are critical to the eyes and face: the following painting sequence and focus is suggested:

1. Under the brow, on the side of the nose bridge, is the darkest point of the face so have the heaviest shadow here.
2. Lay in and shape the eyebrows, thicker in the middle and over the inner eye, and tailing off over the eye outer. Larger figures and busts can add shade/light on eyebrow hair.
3. Down the nose is a darker strip with a specific highlight across the nose bridge. Consider a satin highlight on the bridge and top of the nose for extra sheen. Use eye 'bags' to shape and tidy the eyes.
4. Use a bright red tone under the nose, and dark brown in the nostrils if the scale allows. A redder nose tip indicates that the individual is cold or sick. Use an extreme highlight, perhaps with Satin to amplify this, on top of the nose tip.

5a. The upper lip is a darker maroon, with a thin skin highlight on the upper edge separating the moustache line.
  b. The lower lip is lighter and pinker than the upper with a highlight in the centre.
  c. Larger busts can have shadows indicating that the lips are creased and cracked, using the same maroon tone as used on the upper lip.
  d. Note how the lips taper into the corners, and add a highlight around these.

Consider adding an extra satin sheen with varnish to the lips to indicate wetness.

6. The teeth and inside the mouth should also have varnish to indicate moistness.

Paint the face in three tonal sections with the primary colours Yellow, Red and Blue:

Yellow zone – use for the forehead, brow and temples.
Red zone – use for the cheeks, nose and ears – red indicates that the skin is well oxygenated and full of blood and life; for individuals who are wounded, sick or dying, remove this tone and replace with a greener, paler tone to show pallor.
Blue zone – the beard area – grading colours can include blue or a green/brown tone for blondes.

Tip: First paint the eye on the opposite side to your dominant hand to avoid the nose, then shape the other eye to match. Aim first for symmetry, then shape and design.

Details of Uniform Changes

What a difference a belt can make… This plate provides further detail on adding personal touches to World War I figure projects.

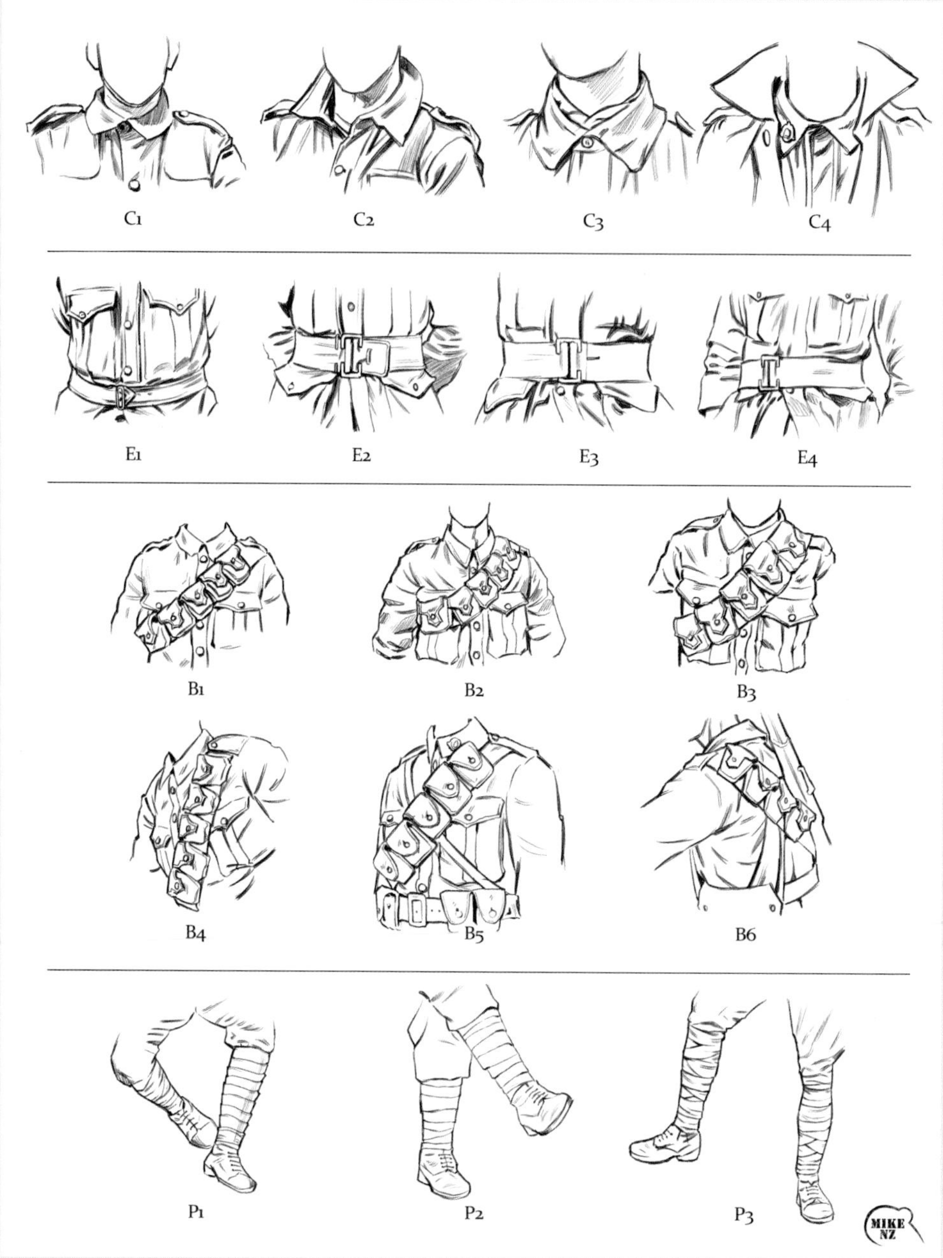

(Continued)

Continued

Collars

Collars (C1–4) help frame the face. Lift the forward edges of a collar even when it is closed (C1), or re-sculpt the collar flaps to be open (C2) or folded up (C4). On smaller figures add a visible shirt collar (C3) with paint, on larger figures use putty.

Belts

Something as simple as how a belt (E1–4) is worn shows personal preferences. The Australian jacket had a soft belt (E1) with a webbing belt covering this. Younger recruits direct from training would follow regulations (E2), whereas veteran soldiers adapted their equipment based on battle experience, for example tucking away or securing any loose flaps on equipment such as the end of their belt (E3–4).

Bandolier Tongues

Bandoliers worn by mounted and artillery soldiers had quick-release tongues on each pouch. Carving out underneath and lifting each of these with a scalpel will accentuate their function. Also consider adding an open flap from plastic card or paper on a few to show they need recharging.

The tongue came in two shapes – the more common angled wedge (B1), and the rounded one seen on earlier New Zealand ex-Territorial troopers (B5). Bandoliers had an adjustable belt and so could be worn tighter up under the right arm (B2), or hanging more loosely down by the side (B4). They could also be simply dropped over the shoulder (B3), although they were supposed to be secured under the left epaulette (B4). Note that ANZAC Light Horse and Mounted Rifle units sometimes had an extra five pouches down their back (B6). This double-sided bandolier was the same as the one a soldier would strap round their horse's neck, as an extra ammunition supply when on patrol.

Infantry Puttees

Infantry puttees were wound up from the ankle to the knee (P1), but in cavalry regiments and artillery (P2) they were wound down from the knee to the ankle. Some were wrapped round in a straight vertical manner, others in a looser crisscross pattern (P3). Always paint with a highlight to emphasize the exposed cloth edge. Remember these soaked up mud and dirt, so would soon become stained, discoloured and encrusted with dust.

Further Details of Uniform Changes

(Continued)

Continued

The Gas-Mask Haversack

A common mistake made by sculptors of World War I British figures is in depicting the gas-mask haversack. These were most often worn reversed, allowing quick access to the gas mask, and also were left partially or fully open with the respirator hose exposed. As a result they add an untidy look to many soldiers (F2–F5). Remove the incorrect flaps and re-sculpt with new flaps using putty or card.

First Aid Dressings

Another example of 'combat sense' was seen late in the war, when New Zealand soldiers took to tying their first aid dressing to the upper left side strap of their mask bags (the dressings are shaded in F1–F3). Some tucked the dressing more securely in place behind the strap (F2). They did this because it was a quick and handy place for right-handed soldiers to grab the dressing in an emergency, especially when wearing a battle jerkin, as the standard location was in a pocket on the inside bottom right of the jacket opening. This new standard position was clearly visible, and everyone in the unit would know where to find it to give first aid to a wounded teammate or enemy casualty.

This small feature can be easily added to a figure or bust with a pellet of putty and some fine thread.

Helmets

Helmets were covered with sacking, some stitched with a drawstring around the crown (F1), or with two- or four-part covers in a buff canvas (F2, F3) or just left bare (F4) to the weather (F5).

Headdress before Helmets

ANZACs on Gallipoli were a ragtag bunch, which was noticeable in the variety of headdress worn. A head covering was seen as a very individual comfort item, before helmets were issued – standard British Service caps were squashed down (G1) or worn backwards (G2, G3) to help when sniping or working, or had a makeshift sun shade sown to the back (G4). Pith sun helmets were worn pushed back (G5) or pulled forwards on the head (G6). The mounted rifles parade standard hat, with folded brim and precise central crease (G8), was more often seen worn down (G7), or with the crease and rim melting under the conditions (G9) , giving the whole hat an unkempt, 'country farmer' look (G10). There was also the woollen cap comforter, a long tubular 'head sock' that could be rolled and folded into a cap (G11).

Uniform Colours: New Zealand 'Lemon Squeezer'

Lemon squeezers.

Manufacturer	Key Points – Source: B. O'Sullivan
1. New Zealand-made fur felt hat	* 8th (Southland) Infantry Regiment badge, cotton serge infantry puggaree, with hooks on the inside under the leather sweat band for a chin strap. * No vents, 6.5cm brim; height 17cm.
2. British-made wool felt hat	* Dated 1918, with a New Zealand Artillery badge, all serge artillery puggaree, with hooks on the inside under the leather sweat band for a chin strap. * Two metal vents on either side of the crown. * Three rows of stitching to the edge of the 6.5cm brim; height 16cm.

(Continued)

Continued

Manufacturer	Key Points – Source: B. O'Sullivan
3. British-made hat, fur felt (not confirmed)	* 1st (Canterbury) Infantry Regiment badge, cotton serge infantry puggaree, hooks on the inside under the leather sweat band for a chin strap. * Two metal vents on either side of the crown. * The edge of the 8cm brim has a fabric trim; height 17cm. **Note:** This hat has a fitting to hold the left side of the brim up, indicating that it was originally made for the Australian Army.
	New Zealand Puggaree colours introduced in 1911: *Field Artillery*: Dark Blue, Red, Dark Blue *All others*: Service Colour (below): Khaki Army Service Corps: White Engineers and Tunnellers: Blue Infantry: Red Mounted Rifles: Dark Green Medical Corps: Cherry Red Veterinary Corps: Purple

PAINTING GALLIPOLI ALLIES

In late April 1915 the ANZACs embarked for Turkey's Gallipoli peninsula as part of a planned Allied invasion to seize the Dardanelles sea passage to Russia. This campaign was the beginning of a colonial brotherhood that would continue to be remembered by future generations.

It was on these shores 100 years later, with my youngest son, that I became more sure of the direction I wanted to follow for my future modelling and painting projects. We were fortunate to be there attending the centennial commemoration at Gallipoli in 2015, and the whole location and event had a profound effect on us both. These finished projects are part of a series of busts and figure conversions that I have planned as a miniature tribute to our forefathers' service. Presented here are details on modelling ANZACs and their allies from the Middle East to the Western Front.

When I saw the Tommy's War 1:10th bust series, their potential for conversion into ANZACs was immediately apparent. Four of the five in the series were snapped up for this purpose, the three featured here, plus an Otago mounted trooper, yet to be painted. The fifth, a Scotsman, was already gone and unfortunately this series is now out of production.

These classic busts were beautifully sculpted by Antonio Meseguer, with separate heads, making them easier to rearrange into alternative versions. These conversions were not very complicated, with simple head swaps on a pair, and Magic Sculpt fine-tuning on all three, with final painting adding to a unique-looking trio.

Despite their being fairly simple compositions, it was a good challenge to explore their different uniforms and how to show the impact of the severe conditions these men endured. More 1:10-scale busts will follow to add to this theme featuring personalities of World War I. In the meantime these three busts will help explain more about modelling subjects from the 1915–16 Mediterranean Front: 'Vic', a young infantryman from a New Zealand Infantry Battalion; 'Robin', a New Zealand non-commissioned officer from Canterbury Mounted Rifles; and 'Abhay', an artillery officer of the Indian Expeditionary G Force.

The three resin bust conversions prepared, ready for painting: here, Robin's face begun with the early stages of flesh base coat and eyes.

'I was keen as mustard, and we had some of the "wild colonial boy" in us when we joined up.' Vic Nicholson reflects in a 1984 documentary.

Private Victor 'Vic' Nicholson

> *I didn't cry, unless Gallipoli was one long cry. If you cried once, you never stopped. There were friends going every day and sometimes every hour of the day, wonderful friends. You cried inwardly, that's all you could do.*
> SOURCE: 'Gallipoli, The New Zealand Story'

Private Victor 'Vic' Nicholson, of the New Zealand Infantry Brigade in Gallipoli, 1915, saw his mate 'Lofty' killed at Quinn's Post, shot through the eye peeping through a peep hole.

As a part of keeping it personal, and to help get inside the character being modelled, it helps to find a suitable individual to represent. This time it was 10/1597 Private Vic Nicholson of 3rd Reinforcements, Wellington Infantry Battalion. He left New Zealand in February 1915 and was involved in battles on ANZAC Cove and later the Western Front, being wounded on both fronts. Vic featured in a 1980s documentary 'Gallipoli, The New Zealand Story'. In it he recounts his story of being a young infantryman at Gallipoli. The quote above was taken from this interview.

Historical Note: Raised from the Dead

PTE. V. J. NICHOLSON,
Wellington Inf. Batt.,
Wounded.

PRIVATE C. H. NICHOLSON,
Medical Corps.
Died of septicaemia following wounds.

Vic and his namesake Claude Nicholson, with whom he shared death for a short time. SOURCE: 'New Zealand's Roll of Honour, 1915' The Auckland Weekly News Illustrated List, *21 October 1915, Auckland, by Wilson and Horton Ltd. Gift of Paul Simmons, 1989. Te Papa (CA000512/001/0021)*

Vic Nicholson was actually 'raised from the dead' after he was recorded in his offical Army personal file as having 'died of multiple compound fractures', and having been 'buried at sea' on 30 October 1915. The next month (28 November 1915) a correction was made to his file that stated: 'Wrongly reported died of wounds, above information refers to 3/913 Private Nicholson NZMC.' Vic had been confused with Private Claude Harold Nicholson, a young medic who had developed septicaemia after major wounds.

Like Fred, the Western Front Lewis gunner earlier in the book, it was to be the pointed felt hat – a 'lemon squeezer' – that would provide a unique feature in this miniature representation of Vic.

Eyes

Pinterest is a good source for suitable images of eye colouring. Remember, on a bust the eyes are large enough not only to allow extra detailing of each part, but also to suggest their oval shape. With highlight and shadow on the sclera the white of the eye is not white – instead, always use a light pink for a more natural look. Shading should also be added below the upper lid and in the lower corners, and highlighting in the mid area to give the idea of their roundness. A blue-grey eye colour

Painting Vic's Head

Important Steps	Key Points: Vic (All paints Jo Sonja unless otherwise stated)
1. Paint the eyes	*Sclera*: VLight Flesh; *highlight*: Titanium White; *shade*: Naples Yellow *Iris*: Payne's Grey + Naples Yellow, + Matisse Midnight Blue for rim and detailing *Pupil*: Raw Umber + Carbon Black *Eyeball edges and blood vessels*: VCadmium Red Umber, VRed Shade * The completed eye is glazed with VGloss Varnish to represent the cornea. *Bags below eyes*: VCadmium Red Umber, Payne's Grey *See also* the update below on Vic's eye colour
2. Paint the face flesh	*Undercoat*: Raw Sienna **Note:** All colouring below is thinned with a blend of VGlazing Medium and VSatin Varnish *Base*: VBeige Red + Raw Sienna *Highlight*: Naples Yellow *Shadows*: Brown Earth, Burnt Sienna, VRed Shade, P3 Flesh Wash *Deep Shadows*: Carbon Black, VGreen Shade *Lips*: VCadmium Umber Red, plus for the bottom lip VBeige Red to highlight and detail *Ears and nose tip*: As for the other skin, then glazed with VRed Shade to add warmth
3. Paint the beard and hair	**Note:** The blonde hair palette benefits from a slight green tinge in shading. *Base*: Raw Sienna *Highlight*: Naples Yellow; *alternative*: P3 Rucksack Tan *Shadows*: Payne's Grey and VCadmium Umber Red, VRed Shade *Deep Shadows*: Raw Umber, VGreen Shade

The flesh palette part way through painting Vic's face, without the JS Payne's Grey used as a softer, neutral blue tone for flesh.

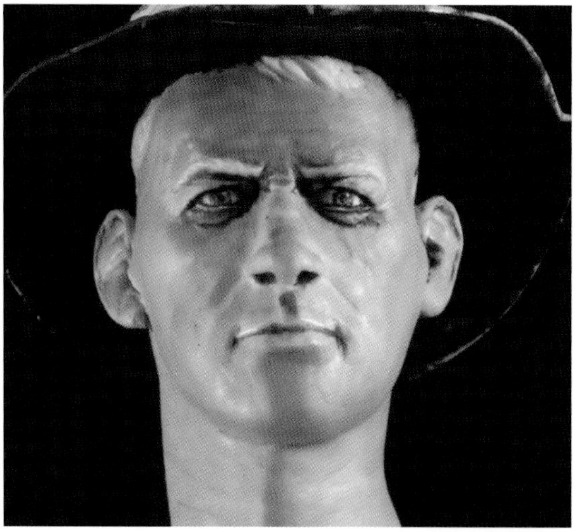

Step 1 of the face: begin with a Raw Sienna undercoat before the eyes are fully painted and detailed.

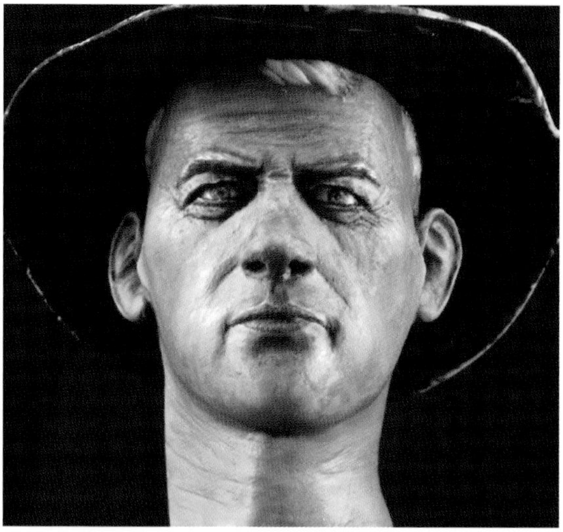

Step 3 of the face: two-thirds done with soft red pink cheeks, helping to show youthfulness, plus warm reddened ears; the chin has a darker beard tone added.

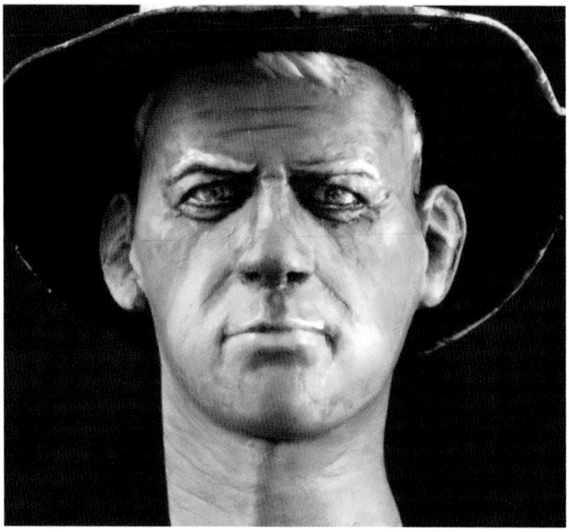

Step 2 of the face: more colour is introduced with yellower, tan tones across the forehead, then down the temples.

was chosen for Vic, primarily to suit the blonde hair I planned – however, when later information was revealed, this turned out to be incorrect! (*See* Reference Note below.)

The final face and hair shows hours of meticulous painting including the eyelashes, sun spots, unshaven chin, ingrained dirt and weary creasing around Vic's eyes.

Reference Note

When this project was first conceived and painted, reference material on individual New Zealand soldiers was difficult to find. Vic was chosen based on a 1984 interview he gave about his time on Chunuk Bair in August 1915. Since then, as part of New Zealand's World War I centennial programme (https://ww100.govt.nz), many of the personnel files and records have been digitized, including the *Auckland Weekly News*, with photos of a number of Gallipoli casualties. Tucked away within these records are photos of a dark-haired, dark-eyed Vic.

Lesson learnt! Always be aware that projects are only as good as the knowledge available at the time. In this case it was decided to keep Vic as he is in miniature, rather than repainting or renaming him. His story is still valid, and, like Charlie later in this book, is representative for all those who served in the Dardanelles campaign.

Smooth skin is more unforgiving when texturing than uniforms; examining the various painting techniques on Vic's face still shows slight roughness.

Bust Face Painting Techniques

Stippling: On the temples, at the sides of the head, are noticeable small spots stippled into the surface to show ingrained dirt and sweat mixed into the pores of the skin. Similar small sun spots and freckles on the face are done in the same careful way, using shadow and highlight colours.

Dabbing: On the cheeks, many small splotches of heavily thinned shadow tones are applied over a lightly shaded base coat. This helps to give a multicoloured variation to the surface, and is also used for effect on Vic's forehead and neck, where a long brush is used to add strips of irregular splotches of colour. The quick-drying characteristic of acrylics is useful to determine how much dabbing is required to build the desired hue, as acrylics always dry much darker than when first applied.

Stibbling: It was important for Vic's face to show some of the ravages of the windswept environment that he was exposed to during a harsh Turkish summer, such as burnt skin and sores. This was done by adding some rougher patches of skin around the upper parts of the cheeks and nose to simulate dirty, peeling flesh. In reality this is hard to see in actual scale, but hopefully it adds to his overall effect in the photos.

All together: stippling, stabbing, stibbling: Vic's rough beard growth is a good place to try these techniques, which starts with a darker base colour – some Green Shade mixed with Raw Sienna. Then carefully build a slight texture using these shadow tones, mixed progressively with a stabbing of Naples Yellow to reveal a few days of rough beard growth, smeared with dust and grime. A tip here is to put as much emphasis on the skin under the beard hair by stibbling in base and flesh shadow colours. A slight texture should be almost invisible to the naked eye, and only really comes out with a magnifier or zoomed-in photographs.

Painting Vic's Clothes

Important Steps	Key Points: Vic (All paints Jo Sonja unless otherwise stated)
1. Paint the shirt collar	*Base*: Payne's Grey + Naples Yellow *Highlight*: Warm White *Shadows*: Carbon Black, Burnt Umber **Note:** The collar needs to be painted before adding the completed head to the torso. Even the bust assembly needs to be thought about, as mistakes can be made with these, too (*see* Charlie)!
2. Paint the lemon squeezer hat	*Undercoat*: Carbon Black *Base*: VEnglish Uniform *Highlight*: AK British Uniform Light *Shadows*: Burnt Umber, Payne's Grey *Sweat salt effect*: Warm White – dabbing is used around the inside brim on the upper and lower surfaces * The hat was begun with a solid black undercoat to make sure there was a visible difference in colour between the hat and the jacket, which had a Raw Umber undercoat. Then dabbed with AK Interactive's WWI British uniform base.
3. Paint the puggaree	*Colour*: Khaki/Red/Khaki for Infantry *Undercoat*: Carbon Black *Base*: AK British Uniform Base *Highlight*: Naples Yellow *Shadows*: Raw Umber
4. Paint the jacket	*Undercoat*: Raw Umber + VEnglish Uniform *Base, Light and Shadow 3 paint set*: AK WWI British Uniform *Deep Shadow*: Carbon Black *Red Trim* – indicates Infantry *Base*: Napthol Red Light *Highlight*: AK British Uniform Light *Shadow*: Raw Umber * A larger brush with a frayed tip was used both to stipple and stibble the large surface areas of the uniform. * A smaller pointed brush was used to tidy and add fine texture detail. * Both brushes are effective in stibbling and stippling – the trick is to have the paint slightly more heavily loaded on the brush, then gently stab the tip and brush sides into the drying paint, thereby pushing the paint on to the surface. This will gradually build up the rougher effect of the battledress serge material. * Once again the aim is not to make this material out of scale, simply to suggest the cloth weave, as can be seen in the real examples shown in the photos in this book.
5. Paint the webbing	*Base*: Raw Sienna *Shadow*: Payne's Grey *Highlight*: Naples Yellow, Warm White
6. Paint the brass fittings	*Base*: P3 Brass Balls *Shadow*: Burnt Umber, VGreen Shade *Highlight*: Pearl White

The lemon squeezer was started by cropping the original sculpt, then the peak was reshaped with putty by figure sculptor Andy Cairns. The bust was also rebuilt with a more casual open collar on the shirt.

Splayed bristles on a larger brush builds texture using stippling and stabbing, then a pointed brush fine-tunes the texture with dabbing and stibbling techniques.

The black lining of the seams is the first step in painting the jacket, followed by texturing effects working from the collar then down the torso using simple uniform mixes.

A rough base coat has been stippled over the jacket leaving a slight sheen that will be matted down with further texturing.

The sides and tips of two different brushes were used to stibble paint, as texture is blended together into a more subtle serge uniform effect.

Stippling is essential to building ribbed webbing texture: choose flat brushes of different sizes and use their sharp edge to apply thicker paint in tiny ridges.

Final additions to create the webbing effect are small sections of base colour, Raw Sienna, stibbled and lightly washed over the sections to represent ground-in dirt.

Repeatedly varying and mixing shadow with highlight colours when stippling the webbing helps emphasize a final 'merged texture' effect.

An intense yet reflective gaze helps give Vic a personality, and this is complemented by various effects that give an authentic look to his clothing.

As much attention was paid to the back of uniform as the front, including nicks in the hat brim to add interest.

Extra highlighting and shadowing was added around worn material to show it breaking down, as on the edging of the hat brim and on the battle-damaged right epaulette.

Trooper Robert 'Robin' Harper, DSO, MC, DCM, MID(3)

Converting the Busts

To represent Robin and Vic at Gallipoli, an exchange of heads was necessary to create this pair of young men. For Vic it was the head and hat adapted from TW10B01 Corporal, East Africa, while TW10B03 Private, Salonika, provided the torso; for Robin it was the opposite. In essence this was a straight head swap from one to the other. Often just changing a head on a bust or figure can give it a whole different look.

This bust conversion was inspired by the story of the Harper brothers, Gordon and Robin (DSO, MC DCM, MID(3) – NZMR Canterbury). They were the youngest pair of siblings from a family of ten, and together with two other brothers served overseas during World War I. Gordon and older brother Eric Harper, a former All Black rugby player, lost their lives serving in Palestine.

Gordon and Robin were key members of the newly created Canterbury Mounted Rifles (CMR) Machine Gun (MG) Section. Robin began as a trooper and would be promoted through the ranks to become the commanding officer of the MG Squadron in Palestine. A unit that was created after Gallipoli was composed of the three MG sections from each of the Mounted Rifles Regiments.

This bust was an ideal candidate to pay homage to Robin at Gallipoli around June–July 1915, when he would have been a corporal (especially since a photograph of him with Gordon showed him smoking a pipe, as was sculpted on the bust). Of particular note for this project to help denote a specific identity were the hat badges, one on the right for the MG section, the other on the left for the CMR. Also, an attempt was made to further reflect the privations of the campaign, in particular the dreadful flies that plagued the soldiers during the long hot summer. These were all but intolerable and would be clearly visible in this scale, so why not try to replicate them? Three were built from small oval blobs of putty, with wings shaped and clipped from clear plastic card.

This was another special project to capture the personality of this young soldier, who would see much more before the end of World War I.

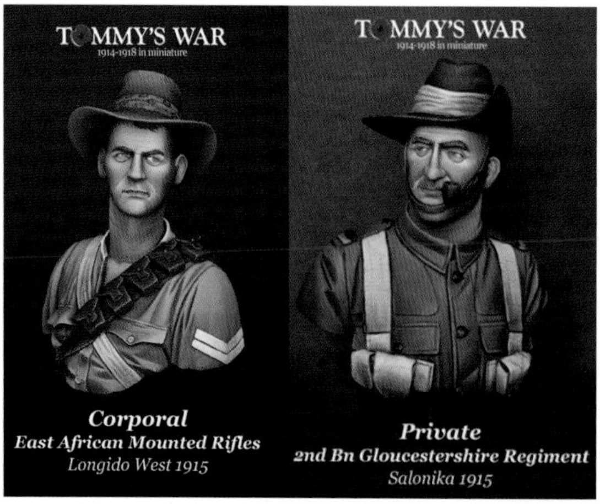

Tommy's War donor busts used in this conversion, and that of Vic, were both painted for the boxart by professional Spanish artist Alex Varela.

Historical Note

The brothers Gordon and Robin were both sheep farmers and were well known for using their rural lifestyle skills when soldiering in Gallipoli and Palestine. For example they had an agreement to always stay in touch using high-pitched dog whistles – as when on a couple of occasions Gordon was injured and signalled to Robin for help.

SOURCE: *Brothers in Arms*, edited by Jock Philips.

Painting Robin

Important Steps	Key Points – Robin (All paints Jo Sonja unless otherwise stated)
1. Paint the eyes	*Iris*: Outer edge Carbon Black, Inner Yellow Ochre and catchlight Warm White. Take care to position and balance the size of the iris. If it is not correct the first time, then continue to repaint it until the look is correct. Remember also that shading from the brim of the felt hat will reduce the reflection directly on the eye. * The eyeball (the sclera) is coated with a thin layer of acrylic Gloss Varnish for a natural, wet look.
2. Paint the flesh	* A variation on the palette used for Vic, with little Beige Red, which was instead replaced with darker brown and tan tones. * Specifically extra Burnt Sienna was applied in the cheek area, Brown Earth in the shadow areas, and Raw Sienna in overall tone. * VBeige Red was used for the ears.
3. Paint the beard	* The beard is more subtle, with less growth, and primarily using Burnt Umber to suggest this.
4. Paint the shirt	*Base*: Payne's Grey *Shadow*: Raw Umber. Carbon Black in the deepest shadows depicts sweat under the arms or in the shirt seams *Highlight*: Naples Yellow, Warm White * A wide variety of shirt colours were worn by the ANZACs at Gallipoli, with personal ones from home replacing army issue ones. Robin had a dark blue-grey one, as seen in photos of him with his brother Gordon. * Other shirt colours could include light grey or blue, olive green or off white.
5. Paint the leather	Chinstrap: Use Citadel (C) colours as main paints as these are thick and dry with a natural sheen. There are three main steps: Base: Carbon Black edging with VBurnt Orange *Shadow*: CRhinox Hide built up in layers *Highlight*: CSnakebite leather, and use a hardened toothpick tip to add scratches and cracking Mounted bandolier: * As the chinstrap in approach, however instead of CRhinox Hide, this was replaced with CMournfang Brown and CSkarag Brown used as main shadowing tones. * Damage and highlights were also added on each pouch using a fine-tipped brush.
6. Paint the hat	*Hat*: as Vic's *Puggaree NZMR Green stripe – base*: Hookers Green; *shadow*: Raw Umber; *highlight*: Naples Yellow *Sewn-on cloth badges:* added with Magic Sculpt *MG Section*: Napthol Crimson over Carbon Black, both lightened with Naples Yellow *CMR checkerboard*: *see* below
7. Detailing the cloth badges	Corporal stripes: These are laid out in three stages: *Backing*: AK WWI British Base with Raw Umber for shadow, and frayed edging lightened with Naples Yellow

(Continued)

Continued

Important Steps	Key Points – Robin (All paints Jo Sonja unless otherwise stated)
	Stripe main tone: Raw Sienna *Central stripe*: Warm White, then divided with Raw Sienna arrow heads using a fine-pointed sable brush Canterbury mounted checkerboard: * Work light to dark – *base*: Warm White * Sketch in Carbon Black squares from left to right, with focus on shape and size. * Fine-tune the detail by mixing Raw Umber into both colours, and add as a White shade/Black highlight mix. * Finalize the pattern with tiny dots of extreme highlights and shadows using the respective base colours. **Tip:** When doing badges make sure to have an actual example, or search for a good clear reference photo. In this scale it is possible to replicate the relatively simple pattern detail. In other cases a representation of the pattern may be enough to simply suggest detail.

Positioning the eyes is always a challenge. Here, Robin's eyes took more than one attempt, as flesh paint residue left after washing from an earlier attempt shows.

Another thin flesh base coat is applied, and basic shadowing tones added. Also see refinements on the bust, such as lifting the bandolier tabs and pocket flaps.

Weathering and texturing are integrated throughout the painting stages, such as here with salt staining under the puggaree and a bloody, grubby collar.

Fine details added to the face in the latter stages of painting include teeth, lips, chin stubble, the warmth of the cheeks and ears, and neck creasing.

The left shoulder shows faded cloth, and painting continues to add this effect across to the right side of the shirt. See also the scratched, sore and paler skin on the chest.

Bandolier flaps were hollowed out underneath with a sharp knife and dental tool. A back pouch flap was replaced with plastic card.

Historical Note

I was fifteen weeks on Gallipoli, and while I was there I had nothing but bully beef and biscuits and flies. You couldn't draw breath through your open mouth but you were swallowing flies, and a lot of the water you drank had to be strained through your teeth. I know this doesn't sound very good ...you know, but it's the truth. We had one ration of bread while I was on Gallipoli and that was one loaf amongst eight of us, so, you know, it was about a mouthful each. That was all we had all the time I was there, bully beef and biscuits. And flies.

Private Bob Needs MM, Otago Infantry Battalion

Details shown are a fly sitting on a small yellow pus sore, redness indicating infection, sweat-soaked armpits, and threading on the corporal stripes.

Abhay, Artillery Officer, G Force

This bust was to be a veteran officer in the New Zealand Native Contingent. Feedback online challenged me to search for a more suitable subject. It was a valuable detour, offering the chance to learn more about a neglected topic rarely presented in miniature. And so Abhay ended up as an artillery officer of the Indian Expeditionary G Force, fighting in Gallipoli in 1915.

The Indian contribution to Gallipoli has long been under-appreciated, and has gone largely unnoticed. With upwards of 16,000 Indian Army soldiers serving, they were a significant part of the Allied offensive attack. Their artillery were the first guns on shore, and last out in December 1915. They were led by both British and Indian officers, and it was one of the latter that this slight conversion of another Tommy's War bust was to become.

Abhay, meaning 'fearless and brave', was an appropriate name for the Indians landing at Gallipoli. They were battle-hardened from

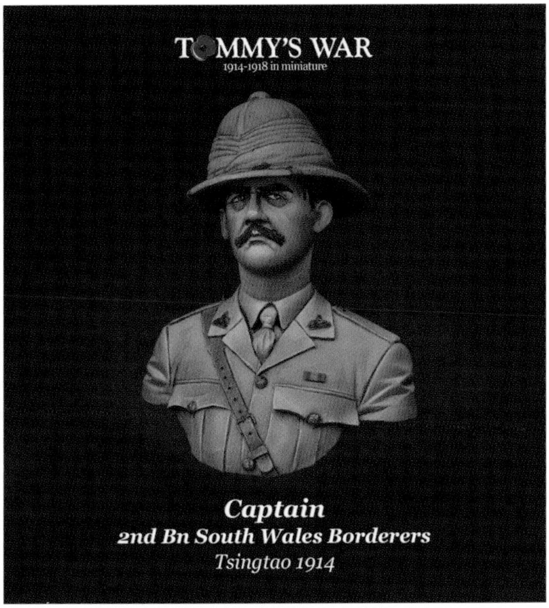

Original boxart bust by Alex Varela, of the bust adapted to an Indian officer serving with invading troops at Gallipoli.

the North-West Frontier, unlike the amateur ANZACs, most on their first trip abroad and naive about war. However, they would soon come to mutually respect and value each other's fighting ability. For the Aussies and Kiwis there was another advantage that came with their new-found friends: a steady, boring diet of bully beef, biscuits and endless tins of apricot jam was quickly supplemented by Indian rations as often as was practical.

The Tommy's War 1:10 bust began as a South Wales Borderers officer with two helmet options – a pith Wolseley and the steel Brodie. Only the pith Topi sun helmet was worn in Gallipoli, and this would also convey the attitude of a confident young officer. Some minor work involved removing his moustache, then using Magic Sculpt around the mouth to accentuate his attitude; also a cloth patch for the Royal Artillery red/blue flash was added on the helmet's left side.

The initial concept was to convert the bust into a Maori officer, and a Native Contingent badge was sculpted for his pith helmet.

Painting Abhay's Olive Complexion Flesh

A primary guide for flesh tones on large figures, and to help add variety in face painting, is *Colour Mixing Recipes for Portraits by* William F. Powell. This inexpensive book is a worthwhile purchase for all figure modellers. It offers recipes to use as a base, with three tone levels (shadow, mid-tone, highlight) plus a greying colour to tone the shadow areas. For Abhay the recipe chosen was the 'Watercolours Olive Skin Tone', with unusual colours in the palette, including blues and green. It helped add something a bit different from the original bust concept, and was certainly a little out of the ordinary. It was a unique challenge to capture a South Asian skin colouring with the tan summer uniform.

Checking painting with the hand; it has become a common practice to provide the background with a photo. Here the bust sits on the workbench amongst the brushes used on the tunic.

Painting Abhay

Important Steps	Key Points – Abhay (All paints Jo Sonja unless otherwise stated)
1. Paint the eyes	*Iris – edge*: Carbon Black; *main colour*: Raw Sienna *Sclera*: Naples Yellow; *highlights*: Warm White **Note:** Ensure a slight yellowing for the eyes with this complexion. *Corners*: Thin wash of VCadmium Umber Red * Finally the eyes are coated with Gloss Varnish.
2. Paint the face	*Base*: Raw Sienna + French Blue *Mid-tones*: Hooker's Green + Alizarin Crimson. These were stibbled on to show mottling with sun spots, especially on the upper cheeks and the fleshy sides beside the nose *Shadows, including the beard area*: Base + Burnt Sienna + Burnt Umber *Highlights*: Cadmium Red Light + Naples Yellow *Hair*: Base – Carbon Black. Lighten with Flesh highlight * All the above paints were blended with VGlazing Medium and Satin Varnish.
3. Paint the shirt and tie	*Shirt – base*: Unbleached Titanium; *shadow*: Raw Umber; *highlights*: Warm White *Tie – base*: Provincial Beige; *shadow*: Raw Umber; *highlights*: Unbleached Titanium **Note:** The tie shadow and highlights pattern were stippled on with a flat brush tip, similar to Vic's webbing above.

(Continued)

Continued

4. Paint the jacket	* Adapted from the Sand Jacket mix used by the original boxart artist Alex Varela. *Base*: Fawn + Olive Green + Brown Earth *Highlights*: Base + SkinTone + Warm White *Shadows*: Base + Raw Umber – used for seams, outlining and deepest creases *Mid-tones*: A mix of washes of Brown Earth and Olive Green * Colours are laid down with a medium flat brush (7mm) in successive thin layers, then given a final touch-up using a pointed #2 sable for smaller creases, edges and stitching.
5. Paint the helmet	*Top – base*: Yellow Oxide + Raw Umber; *shadow*: Raw Umber; *highlights*: Naples Yellow + Unbleached Titanium *Underside – base*: Olive Green; *shadow*: Raw Umber; *highlights*: Sap Green * Similar brushwork was used as in the jacket; however, dabbing was used to vary light, shadow and weathering.
6. Paint the leather	*Chinstrap*: As Robin's, using Citadel acrylics Sam Browne: *Base*: VOrange Brown *Shadow*: CRhinox Hide + CCaliban Green. Shadowing was pooled on with dabbing to give a deeper transparent sheen for polished leather *Highlights*: Base + Naples Yellow – used for the main highlighting on the upper edging and cracking around the buckle

Abhay looking smart in his tropical uniform, with special attention paid to getting smoother effects on his cotton clothing.

Darker skin tones are an interesting challenge; using earthen tones helps with this. An artillery flash is added to the sun helmet.

Sculpting the 'Kalgoorlie' Bust

Steve commented he has always had an avid interest in World War I. This stemmed from learning that his paternal grandfather's half-brother Albert Leadley served throughout the whole of the war as a driver in the Royal Field Artillery. He was invalided due to a fractured skull after being kicked by a mule at Mons, then re-enlisted in the North Staffs Regiment. He had been due to go to Gallipoli, via Egypt, but actually ended up serving in Mesopotamia, then Palestine, where he saw the war out.

Steve was originally a sculptor and modeller for Royal Doulton. He has been involved with military modelling for as long as he can remember, and started working on his own range of busts for subjects that were somewhat niche. The inspiration for this bust initially came from watching Peter Weir's *Gallipoli* and *The Lighthorsemen*, along with a BBC series called *All the King's Men* featuring David Jason – as well as after reading countless books and references about the campaign.

Steve envisaged a young digger caught out in No Man's Land in Gallipoli in 1915, after an assault – out of ammo, sheltering in a shell hole, scared and straining to look over the edge in the hope of a friendly face to rescue him. Steve had already worked on a couple of other busts commercially in this scale. He was fortunate to have the Staffordshire Regiment Museum at Lichfield close by, so he could check on webbing and shirts. The remainder of the research was done via the internet and from his own collection of books.

The master sculpture is multicoloured as Steve used a mix of grey/green Milliput, with detailing in a mixture of Duro/Greenstuff. He also primed the bust as he progressed with Mr Surfacer 500 to hide the blends, then overpainted in grey auto primer to check the surfaces. The bust itself has a choice of two hat versions, one with the brim down and one with it up, pinned by the Australian 'Rising Sun' cap badge. The hat was probably the most difficult part of the sculpt as he had to balance scale thickness with strength for production, especially on the folded version.

The webbing pouches were sculpted with the flaps open to indicate that the soldier was out of ammo, which meant sculpting both parts of the press studs. Steve also added texture to the webbing and the straps, as these had a distinctive woven pattern to them. For the texture

The sculpture shows Milliput and primer, originally with only the top ammo pouches (L), then Duro/Greenstuff mix used for detailing and the lower row of pouches (R).

Hat options: the flap up with the AIF badge (L), and down (R). Brims were cut from thin aluminium sheet, and covered with a thin rolled sheet of Duro for thickness.

The master bust fully prepared and ready for casting by ModelCellar, with a good example of the simple Australian World War I slouch hat band, clip and air vents.

pattern he applied a fabric tape, then sealed this with thinned PVA.

The sculpt itself appeared as the subject of a step-by-step on the PlanetFigure forum back in 2011, and Steve was fortunate to have many of the members offer advice and details throughout its design, including the suggestion of adding exposed identity discs. The completed bust master was purchased by the US company ModelCellar, and is still in production.

Painting note: Much of this larger bust was treated in a similar way to Vic and Robin. The difficulty was to show the soldier in a final desperate situation as Steve originally intended: a frightened, filthy, sweaty young Aussie sheltering in a trench with little to do except await the outcome of the battle.

'Kalgoorlie' – Light Horseman, The Nek

By July–August the ANZAC troops' dress sense had become a non-issue. Increasingly they picked up names such as 'The Naked Army', and 'Scarecrows', alluding to their random, mixed dress from clothing worn out from battle, as well as the overall conditions and shortages on ANZAC Cove. Long trousers were cropped into shorts, and shirts lost their sleeves or were replaced with items sent by family at home. As a result the colour of shirts varied too, from dirty white to dark blue and lots of different shades in between. This bust represents a typical young Australian at this time, and was sculpted by Steve Leadley, aka 'Valiant' on Planet Figure.

Historical Note

Identity discs, known as 'meat tags' by the soldiers, were issued for every individual soldier. These small discs were the means to identify him or her in the event of their death. Early in the war soldiers were issued with only one aluminium ID disc, but aluminium eventually became impossible to obtain, so an asbestos fibre one was made to replace it. Soldiers also began the informal practice of adding a second tag, so their identity would not be lost from their body after the original tag was taken. This was made official in an Army order in 1916, when it was deemed that the 'Disc, Identity, No. 1 Green' tag would be left with the body, and the 'No. 2 Red' tag would be collected to be used for record keeping.

Comparing bust scales: Robin 1/10 (180mm) and Kalgoorlie 1/8 (200mm), showing how much extra area there is to paint and texture.

Painting the Aussie Soldier

Important Steps	Key Points (All paints Jo Sonja unless otherwise stated)
1. Paint the eyes and flesh	* Similar to Vic, however more VBeige Red is added to give a flushed pink tone. * Red Crimson mixed with Satin Varnish was also added to the corner of the eyes and in a small splashed pattern on the right cheek wound. Jo Sonja Satin Varnish dries with more gloss than Vallejo varnish, so is useful for a thin, watery, wet blood effect. * More pronounced sweat on the temples and brows is done with tiny drops of VGloss Varnish and Medium. * For the grazed cheek, VCadmium Umber Red was used for dried blood, with Red Crimson thinned with Gloss acrylic medium for oozing blood.
2. Paint the beard and hair	* As Vic. * A lighter beard growth effect was created, to show youthfulness.
3. Paint the shirt	*Grubby filth on shirt: Jo Sonja acrylics* *Base*: Warm White *Highlight*: Extremes only Warm White with Titanium White *Shadow*: Base + Raw Sienna and Raw Umber *Sweat staining*: Shadow + Payne's Grey. This was added down the front of the shirt, on the edges of, and under the sleeves. Various tones are achieved with these colours mixed in using Vallejo Glazing Medium to blend the edges together.
4. Paint the webbing	* As Vic's webbing, with extra shadow washes to help bring out the detail of the tape Steve added to the webbing straps.

(Continued)

Continued

Important Steps	Key Points (All paints Jo Sonja unless otherwise stated)
5. Paint the hat	* As Vic's hat. *Hat band*: Provincial Beige; *shadow*: Raw Umber; *highlights*: Naples Yellow * Australian felt hats had a single band with a rib of stitching at the top and bottom. * 'Kalgoorlie' was added freehand using Raw Umber. The hat band colours were lightly brushed through it to show it fading and wearing off.
6. Painting the metals	*Base*: Carbon Black *Buttons*: Silver printer's ink with W&N Raw Umber oils for shading *Brass*: Gold printer's ink with Rembrandt Burnt Sienna and Raw Umber mixed in for shading. Highlights include a tiny dash of Silver mixed with Gold **Note:** W&N Liquin is used to help the printer's ink flow and as a drying agent.
7. Paint the ID discs	*Red disc*: Burnt Sienna *Green disc*: VOlive Green *Shadow for both discs*: Raw Umber

Skin painting requires the patient layering of various tones. Here, a second stage of laying on thinned red and browns looks scary, but keep telling yourself to 'trust the process'.

Continued work focused around the central face area, using a full spectrum of texturing effects, with smaller and thinner layers of paint.

Finally the face emerges and the process begins again, with his stretched neck. A third layer was built up from thin Vallejo Beige Red.

Work started on the shirt from the inside outwards with a mid-tone base colour, followed by gradual layers to add light and shadow.

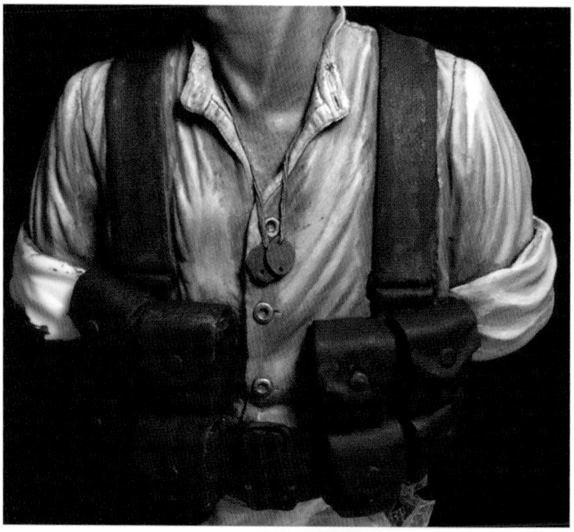

The grotty white shirt is stressed with earth colours scrubbed in, along with darker neutral tones to simulate sweating under the webbing and around the chest.

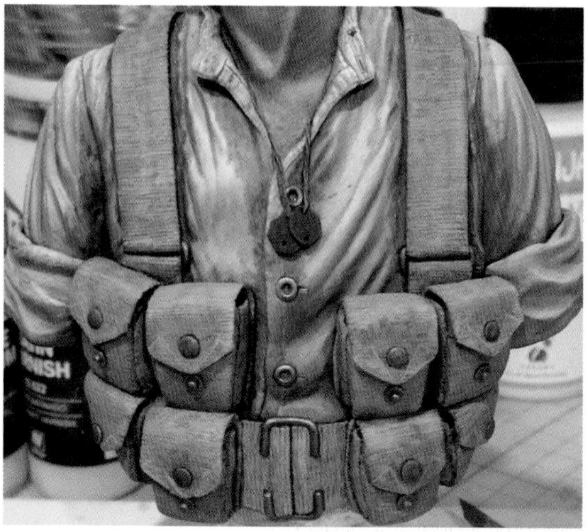

The finished webbing texture, dulled brass and shiny metal buttons all add a structured feel to the torso, complete with a splash of colour from the identity discs.

Beads of sweat dribble down the side of the soldier's face, added with dabs of gloss varnish and thin vertical lines of gloss acrylic medium.

Once again the back view has areas of interest built in, such as Steve's neat, tape-covered webbing, as well as painted-on shirt tears and rips.

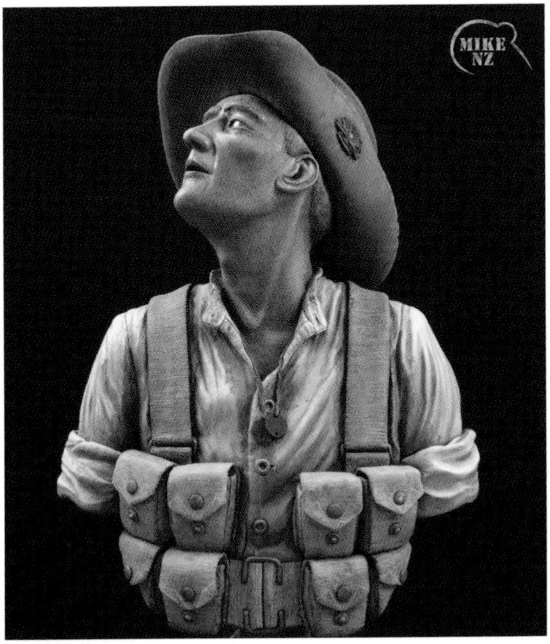

Even at this scale, high resolution photos often emphasize detail that is just not visible without a magnifying lens and a good light source.

The cheek graze adds drama, and the scrawled 'Kalgoorlie' identifies the soldier's West Australian mining town home, inspired by a background character in Peter Weir's film Gallipoli.

Uniform Colours: New Zealand Western Front Uniform

Manufacturer	Key Points – Source: Malcolm Thomas
1. Front	* 1902 English service dress jacket issued to a private soldier of 9th (Hawke's Bay) Company, part of the Wellington Infantry Regiment (WIR). * Felt hat with infantry puggaree. * Brass Unit cap badge – Red Deer, Roman numeral 'IX' unit number, and 'Kia Toa' ('Be Brave') motto, King's Crown and Fernleaf wreath. * The collar badges are miniatures of the cap badge without the fern wreath. * Brass 'NZ Forces Southern Cross' buttons. * Gas-mask haversack is secured in the 'alert' position with the owner's personal detail stencilled on in black paint. * 1908/13 bayonet, without the curved quillon seen on earlier models, and the entrenching tool handle stowed together on the left hip.
2. Right back angle	1908 clothing webbing has attached: * Felt-covered water bottle with the cork fastened by string. * Small haversack worn as a backpack. * Entrenching tool cover.
3. Right front side	* New Zealand Rifles 'NZR' brass shoulder titles. * Cuff badge showing three years of overseas service for 1916–1918.
4. Back	* Gas-mask haversack strap around the collar. * Cloth patch for the 1st Battalion 1/WIR. The unit served on the Somme in 1916, Messines and Passchendaele in 1917, and in the Spring Offensive in 1918. * The backpack has a chipped enamel mug.
5. Other uniform items not shown	* Mark 1 steel helmet normally worn in action – a lemon squeezer would be worn when safe and out of the line. * Infantry trousers were full length, lower half tightened against the leg before puttees were applied. * New Zealand Infantry ORs ('Other Ranks') boots were black. Officers wore brown.

New Zealand Western Front 1.

New Zealand Western Front 2.

New Zealand Western Front 3.

New Zealand Western Front 4.

CORPORAL 'CHARLIE' TOWN BUST

Author's Note

The campaigns of 1917 have special significance to me as seven of my great uncles and cousins were with the New Zealand troops at this time. One was wounded by shrapnel and sent home; two were repeatedly injured, though returned to the front after recovering from each event. One was sent home to die after contracting pneumonia in the trenches, and one was killed by artillery fire on the first day of Ypres on 31 July 1917. Another one was wounded; he remained in the field and was killed when taken as a prisoner of war. The last one was killed during the Messines offensive.

Many more New Zealanders were to become casualties, with their worst day being at Passchendaele on 12 October 1917. Therefore it was these men I wanted to remember with my model, as a representative for them all. I chose Charlie Town as this individual to represent the rest, to symbolize an ANZAC on the Western Front at this time.

Naked Army (ANZAC figures) and sister company Khaki Army (US figures) provide paintable, resin-cast model kits similar to the more familiar smaller-scale figures, but in 1:6 (300mm) and 1:10 (150mm) large scales. The figures are designed and sculpted by owner Scott Edwards and his team. These model kits are adapted from the company's presentation range, which are produced as bronze and faux-bronze sculptures. These have a highly technical and historically accurate 'hyper-real' sculpting style, with some even becoming larger-than-life sculptures that have been used as memorials in Australia.

The kits are made of a hard, marble-like polystone resin that takes putty and paint well without the need for a primer. Each figure presents a heroic portrayal of servicemen and women in miniature, consistent with the company's primary aim to honour those who served in the nineteenth and twentieth centuries.

It is challenging to paint convincingly in this scale as the size is unforgiving, with every brush-stroke and mistake obvious, not to mention the large sections to paint, many bigger than an entire 1:32-sized subject. However, it also gives an opportunity to push skills into a range of textures and effects when the figure is tackled as a series of individual projects – for example helmet, face, webbing, weapons and so on.

An impressive feature that comes to light as you add colour to these figures is the level of detail. The white polystone is a robust-looking material, where much of the subtle detail of the masters is not immediately visible. This detail is geared to being revealed by the bronzing process, in which most of these are produced as hot or cold cast bronzes.

Historical Background: ANZACs on the Western Front

Soon after the successful evacuation from the Turkish peninsula in December 1915, the ANZAC forces were split in two. Most of the mounted units were sent into the cavalry-friendly open desert terrain of Palestine, their aim being to prevent enemy forces taking control of this strategically important region, especially the Suez Canal. The remaining units, including infantry, artillery and support troops, were despatched to Europe to bolster the Allied war effort, which was flagging under the increasing losses from the destructive effects of modern warfare.

Upon arrival in France in early 1916 a reformatted ANZAC Division was created. Into this, many new troops arrived, reinforcements from home inspired by tales of Gallipoli and eager to 'do their bit'. These included the recently established units of the New Zealand Rifle Brigade (NZRB) – The Earl of Liverpool's Own, comprising four battalions. By 1917 these men had been exposed to the perils of life on the Western Front – but worse was still to come for them, with involvement in the major offensives at Messines and Passchendaele.

Charlie in his 'Sunday best' as he appeared in the casualty list after his death. This does not show the toll of two years fighting in France and Flanders.
ONLINE CENOTAPH

Corporal Charles Edward Town

Blue-eyed, fair-haired Charlie was a big man for his time at six feet tall. He was a broken-nosed, barrel-chested labourer from Parnell, Auckland. He joined A Company of the 3rd Battalion New Zealand Rifle Brigade aged thirty-two in late 1915, and arrived in France with them in 1916. During his time there he was wounded and received the Military Medal (MM) for his part in surviving New Zealand's darkest hour.

HISTORICAL NOTE

In recognition of his bravery, Charlie Town was awarded the Military Medal, as the following citation from the *London Gazette*, 28 January 1918, records:

> *For conspicuous gallantry and devotion to duty during the attack on the Passchendaele Ridge on the 12th October 1917. He did exceptionally fine work on the flank of his Battalion as No. 1 of a Lewis Gun team, when an enemy counter-attack showed signs of developing. He showed great gallantry throughout the day.*
> Military Medal. 25/1150 TOWN, Charles Edward

Though promoted to corporal after this battle, Charlie would sadly not live to take his award home to show his widowed mother as he would be killed in action on the Somme in March 1918. He is commemorated at the New Zealand Memorial, Grevillers British Cemetery, Pas-de-Calais, France.

The bust is not intended as an exact likeness of Charlie, instead more a portrayal in memory of him and the couple of thousand young Kiwi men killed on those few days in early October 1917. This version also illustrates a 'Dink' – depicting what he and his mates may have looked like during a lull from the mud, grime and action in late 1917/early 1918. ('Dink' is short for the 'Fair Dinkums', a New Zealand slang term for 'real soldiers'. It was given to NZRB as a term of genuine esteem. Source: *The Official History of the New Zealand Rifle Brigade*.)

The basis of the conversion is the 1:6-scale Naked Army kit (NA111) – Australian Lewis Gunner France 1918. There are two head options in the box – the Australian soft felt slouch hat, or a British-style steel helmet. The latter was chosen to help convey the imminence of battle.

The bust torso is dressed in the Australian jacket, and although ANZAC uniforms are similar, there are still a number of modifications to convert this into a New Zealander wearing the British service dress. The Australian uniform was of domestic design and manufacture, whereas the New Zealand uniform was primarily British standard issue either made in Britain or locally. Photographs of a surviving jacket with equipment owned by New Zealand militaria expert and author Malcolm Thomas were crucial in getting the detail, textures and look of this 'Dink' correct.

The original kit bust is an Australian, apparent from his buttoned cuffs, exterior jacket pockets and pleated back seams.

The massive size of Charlie relative to other ANZAC mates helps give a sense of his scale. Left to right*: Australian 75mm, Ed 54mm, NZMR 150mm (1/10).*

Charlie Conversion

Important Steps	Key Points
1. Sculpt the broken nose	Rework the original nose with Magic Sculpt to add more character.
2. Reshape the neck	A major learning exercise! Explained in gruesome detail with photos below.
3. Add the coarse hessian helmet cover	Made from an old handkerchief – detail below.
4. Rework the Australian uniform	Removed: * High collar on the jacket * AIF 'Sun burst' collar badges * 'Australia' shoulder titles and unit shoulder badge * Lewis Gunner qualification badge scraped off the upper right sleeve. New Zealanders wore this badge on their lower left sleeve. Reworked and/or filled: * Open button tops and cuffs * Jacket's exposed hem stitching * Separate lower coat pocket
5. Add the shirt collar	Use a rolled strip of Magic Sculpt putty to create the collar, with a button made from a small disc of putty.
6. Rebuild and add NZ uniform detail	* NZRB brass shoulder titles from Scale Link etched lettering * Added from Magic Sculpt putty: * Front jacket top straps * Right-hand closed cuff * Rounded brass-button tops * Integral pockets * NZRB 3rd Battalion shoulder flash * Jacket back padded seam * Shoulder sleeve seams * Damaged left cuff with exposed internal hem
7. Make a wrist bandage for the wounded left wrist	Detail below.
8. Build the enamelled steel mug	Made from a chapstick lid, with a Magic Sculpt handle and a new strap to secure it to the pack.

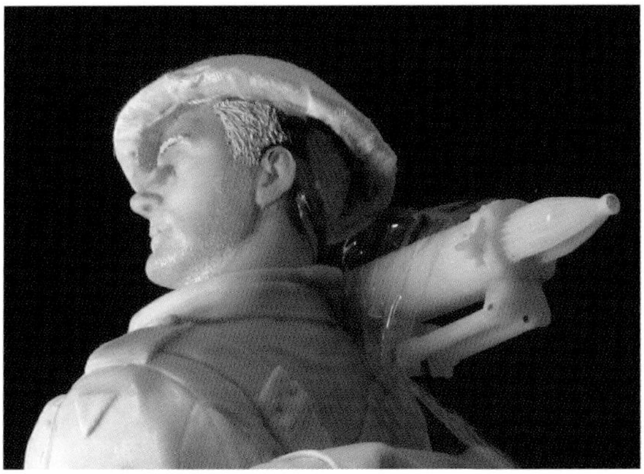

Naples Yellow oil paint was applied with a brush and toothpick for the hair and beard area.

Bust ready for painting with various modifications including redesigned jacket features and detailing of the Lewis gun.

Painting of the face used an unconventional approach, laying in a range of colours one after the other, aiming for a blotchy and realistic effect of a guy who has been through a tough scrape (this approach has now been standardized – see the explanations of the painting techniques earlier). Particular attention was paid to a flushed redness on the cheeks, as well as minor scratches and grazes. Charlie's flesh was finished with small splashes and washes of earth, mud and shade colours using a frayed brush. This 'battle damage' was kept discreet on the face as he would have rubbed and washed his face clean, though roughly, with some muddied water before his cigarette.

Charlie Painting

Important Steps	Key Points (All paints Jo Sonja unless otherwise stated)
The palette for Charlie was adapted from William F. Powell's Caucasian Medium Tones and Golden Brown fair hair recipes. This book really helps in getting you started with an interesting mix, especially in bigger scales.	
1. Lay in oils for the beard and hair	* Squeeze out a large blob of W&N Naples Yellow oil paint (approx. 0.5cm round) on to a non-absorbent surface, such as a plastic disposable tray or old credit card. * Apply thick oil paint 'paste like' to the hair area using a flat brush, like a spatula, layering it on thickly. * Leave the paint to settle for about 30–60 minutes. * Once applied, oils will still take a couple of days to dry at room temperature which allows them to be worked. * If the climate is hot and dry, paint can be kept moist and workable by storing the project in the refrigerator. * A similar approach was used for the stubble, except the oil paint was stippled on, instead of thick oil being laid on.
2. Texture the stubble and hair	* This is done by texturing the oil paint directly, once applied on to the resin, using a fine brush and sharpened toothpick. * Tease the 'hair' using a toothpick tip, and leave to set for about 12 to 24 hours. * Fine-tune and tease the 'hair' again with a toothpick. You can also try a drawing pin or needle. * Leave to dry fully for at least 72 hours.
3. Paint the hair	* Oils and acrylics have been tested on dry oil hair and do work. * The preference is acrylics, with a small amount of Vallejo Satin to provide hair sheen. These avoid the risk of using an oil thinner, which could break down the fine texture.

(Continued)

Continued

Important Steps	Key Points (All paints Jo Sonja unless otherwise stated)
	Base: Yellow Ochre + Naples Yellow + Burnt Sienna *Shadows*: Raw Sienna + Burnt Umber + Burnt Sienna *Highlights*: Base + Naples Yellow
4. Paint the eyes	*Whites*: VLight Flesh. Thinned Napthol Crimson Red and satin varnish in corners *Iris*: Payne's Grey + Naples Yellow *Pupils*: Carbon Black, catchlight from VLight Flesh * The corners and shape of the eyes were coloured with Flesh Mid Tones. * The eyes were finished with acrylic Gloss Varnish.
5. Paint the flesh tones	*Base*: Cadmium Yellow Light, Plum Pink *Shadows*: *Warm*: Base + Burnt Sienna, VCadmium Umber Red *Cool*: Base + Carbon Black *Greying*: Base + Sap Green Mid Tones: Base + Plum Pink + Napthol Red *Highlights*: *First*: VMedium Flesh + Yellow Ochre + Naples Yellow *Second*: Naples Yellow, SkinTone Base, VLight Flesh All stages were mixed with VGlaze Medium and VSatin Varnish to create a soft skin sheen, as face tones were built up using transparent glazes. *Scratches and dried blood*: VCadmium Umber Red, Naphthol Crimson *Mud and grit splashes*: VFlat Earth and Payne's Grey
6. Paint blood and dress a wound	*Dried Blood*: VCadmium Umber Red, VRed Shade Wash, Burnt Umber, Burnt Sienna. These were stippled in with muddy uniform colours, around the wound and bruised fingers. *Moist blood*: W&N Burnt Sienna + White Spirits *Wet blood*: Linseed oil mixed with Rowney Alizarin Crimson + W&N Burnt Umber *Wound dressing*: Made from a pellet of Magic Sculpt, smoothed and shaped to the wrist. *Bandage*: Came from a flesh-coloured sticky tape sold in chemists for minor cuts. This was wrapped in a rough-and-ready way around the wound dressing. *Paint* for dressing and bandage: *White*: Unbleached Titanium *Yellow*: VIce Yellow *Bandage*: Provincial Beige

Blood and Wounds – a Delicate Matter…

Charlie's left wrist has a bandaged flesh wound, with a trickle of fresh blood and fluid seeping down his wrist from under the bandage. The fingers on his right hand have dried blood between them to suggest he held the wrist wound before bandaging; they also show bruising and scratched

A decent Kiwi bruiser, his 'rugby' nose inspired by portraits of Charlie and ancestor Walter Francis. Note also the handkerchief helmet cover.

The face was completed after many hours of texturing, especially dabbing around the reddened cheeks and stippled stubble.

knuckles. All this helps to indicate the hand-to-hand scuffles he had just been involved in.

The author helped translate Sergey Popovichenko's excellent article in Mr Black SMH Figure Modelling #10 'Portraying Realistic Blood

The wound dressing was made from Magic Sculpt shaped to the wrist, then covered with a bandage from sticky tape.

in Miniature'. Sergey recommends studying bloody clothing, boxing and wrestling injuries, and wounds on the internet, which will help with visualizing colouring, and what blood looks like on different surfaces. It will also help guide an approach to painting dried, moist, coagulating and wet blood. Sergey's article advises that there are more brown tones than red ones on wounds. Experimenting with different thinners, mediums and paint types helps achieve realism with this complex effect. However, when it comes to representing blood, remember that subtlety is critical, and that a little goes a long way in telling a story of warfare. The suggestion of a gash or injury is often more effective than graphic bleeding.

Helmet Cover

When making the helmet, a feature was to show a worn sacking cover with pencil graffiti, as seen on an August 1917 photo of NZRB 3rd Battalion out of the line, having lunch and reading German propaganda. This type of graffiti seems to have been an unofficial Kiwi way of 'tagging' who they were and where they had been. There are other examples of British army units doing this too. Small touches like this help to differentiate figures, giving them a deeper sense of place and time.

New conversion details include magazine rivets made from foil using a jeweller's awl, a new collar, and new buttons and jacket shoulder patches.

Making the Helmet

Important Steps	Key Points
1. Make the helmet cover	* The helmet covering started life as a white cotton handkerchief, with a tight woven, coarse texture. * Cut out a large circle, then tack in place with superglue. * Fine yellow nylon thread helps to represent the twine drawstring used to secure Charlie's home-made cover. * Cut the thread into short lengths, supergluing each end, then carefully position with tweezers.
2. Paint the first coat	* Painting began with a heavy soaking of VGreen Ochre, mixed with Secret Weapon Yellow Earth pigment, water and white glue. * As this mix dries it stretches the cover taut. * Leave to dry overnight.
3. Shade the helmet	* Wash the helmet sides and under the rim with a mix of Raw and Burnt Umbers, heavily thinned with Glaze Medium. * Leave to dry thoroughly for a couple of hours.
4. Paint the second coat	* Add a further wash using more Secret Weapon Yellow and Dark Earth pigments flowed on with natural methylated spirits (available from a chemist). * This dries very quickly as the spirits evaporate.
5. Create a muddied effect	* With a clean piece of Blu Tack, dab randomly around and over the helmet cover top. * This will lift some of the pigment from the painted cover, leaving an uneven, muddied sacking pattern.
6. Add graffiti	* Personal graffiti – 'NZ', 3 Battalion's triangle unit symbol, 'RB' – was scribed on with a fine HB pencil. * Pencil was also used to show the bare metal edging on the helmet rim, appearing inside a tear in the cover.

A Hiccup! Coaching from a Master Modeller Fixes an Error

Sharing progress online to seek feedback throughout these larger projects is invaluable. This is especially important when modelling in isolation, as it becomes vital to rely on others to provide an external perspective, which can be lost when fully absorbed in the project. What we want to achieve may be inaccurate or incorrect, as we only know what our experience or references may say. Most modellers in online forums tend to be supportive, and if asked will offer suggestions on paint colours; however, tips on anatomy are especially valued.

Initially the intention with Charlie was to capture a certain look – his head twisted sharply to the left, looking directly at the viewer. The Lewis gun would frame him from behind. When Charlie's head and helmet were completed, they were glued in place, then shared on PlanetFigure. The feedback from others, including master sculptor Mike Good, was that the head position 'looked wrong'. The initial reaction to this advice was resistance, to avoid making the necessary changes – too much work has been done, it would be too difficult to correct. However, after further reflection the decision was made to go ahead, so the completed head was severed, a new neck built and the head repositioned.

Mike Good's coaching was essential throughout this phase. He patiently offered his expert guidance over many days, all in plain view of others on the forum. It took three attempts to make the necessary change, with many hours of repositioning, carving and filling until it was suitably altered. The head twist was slighter, Charlie's Adam's apple remained central to his chest, the back of the neck curved in, and the head was tilted forwards. All these changes resulted in a more pleasing, natural pose. Once Charlie's head was sorted it was possible to add a new shirt collar from Magic Sculpt, then all the paintwork damaged during this repair work was touched up.

The awkward angle of the head can be seen in this original position. On the shoulder is the 3rd Battalion triangle formation badge.

This was a lesson in never getting ahead of yourself without a second opinion. The head was glued in place, then painted without checking its position.

A more sensible approach is to add a rod into the head so its position can be tested and painted.

Comparing the converted NZ figure with the original Aussie kit figure, including the reshaped neck. The 'A' on the Australian's shoulder shows that he was a Gallipoli veteran.

TIP

It always pays to keep the head separate from the body, using brass wire or similar, so the final position can be adjusted when the parts come together.

Painting Uniform Texture, Mud and Brass

Painting uniform textures is always approached with an experimental learning cycle of plan, do, check, act:

* Plan an approach: paints, brushes, thinner and medium.
* Do some painting: different strokes, dots, dabs.
* Check results: blended or not blended? Is the surface texture OK?
* Act on what you see: if it looks fine, keep doing it; if not, adjust, try again.
* Then repeat for each step until you are satisfied with the results.

Blending Medium and Flat Base proved essential to building texture patterns and giving the paint a flat, muddied finish.

Painting Charlie's Uniform

Important Steps	Key Points
1. Undercoat the uniform area	Use thin, solid coats of Carbon Black applied evenly over the uniform area.
2. Paint the base colour	* Overpaint by stippling the base colour: VEnglish Uniform + Raw Sienna. * Apply thin paint heavily for the uniform and webbing with a mix of W&N Blending Medium + a drop of Tamiya X-21 Flat Base. * The paint mix remains workable for an hour or two and is applied in a deliberate blotchy effect with the largest of two flat brushes in a downward motion.
3. Texture the base with shadows and highlights	*Shadows*: *First* – Base + Raw Umber *Second* – Raw Umber + Carbon Black

(Continued)

Continued

Important Steps	Key Points
	Highlights: Base + Naples Yellow * When painting large areas of uniform, work is often done with three brushes at a time to blend and work up texture in the acrylics. Brushes and serge uniform texture: * For painting serge material, the brush should stay flat, with a slight even split off the bristle ends. It needs to give neat groups of spots or rows for webbing, which will provide the basis for textures. The South Korean Style × modelling brushes consistently work well. * Initial irregular spotting is followed by a cheaper 'no name' flat brush with a slight burr or splay at the end – more precise for a dot or stripe approximately 0.75mm. * Touching up and shadowing is done with Vallejo sables 0 and 1 – these have good points and are inexpensive, but will do the job.
4. Add dried mud	* A smaller, flat brush with an angled, heavily worn, bristle end adds an authentic variety to this effect. * Painting begins by stippling and dabbing irregular blotches of Base mud colours – VGreen Ochre, VLight Mud, mixed with a little extra Flat Base. * Highlight the top and edges with Naples Yellow to suggest drier mud. * Be aware that Flat Base may show through as white spots. These can be easily blended and toned out with a fresh Uniform or Mud Base mix. * Finally apply random mixes of Naples Yellow, Raw Umber and Carbon Black. This can take quite a while, but the result should be a convincing messy, muddy, grainy effect of a filthy battledress. * The emphasis for mud is on the jacket front, sleeves, cuffs and elbows. These are places that would naturally become covered with mud as Charlie manoeuvred to get into good firing positions.
5. Paint the brass	*Undercoat*: Citadel Zambesi Desert *NZRB blackened brass*: Tamiya × 19 Smoke + VUmber Shade Wash *Brass highlights*: Gold Acrylic pen fluid (printer's ink) *Dull brass tarnish*: VBrass + Hookers Green + VAcrylic Satin Varnish *Bright brass*: Jo Sonja Pearl White mixed with VBrass + VSepia (*See* detail below.)

More on Brass: Buckles, Badges, Buttons and Shoulder Titles

The original plan was to leave off the Rifle Brigade collar badges, simply saying they popped off in action. However, in research it was found that a great-great uncle on the Western Front was actually charged and disciplined for losing one collar badge. So the feeling at this stage was that soldiers felt a sense of pride in turning out correctly as a member of the NZRB. They were 'encouraged' to hang on to their badges, more so than in Gallipoli, where badges were commonly absent from uniforms. The NZRB aligned themselves with the historic UK Rifle Brigade, adopting their blackened buttons and the badges associated with them.

Magic Sculpt was used to sculpt miniature representations of the pair of collar badges, based on a real example in the author's collection.

Shoulder titles were also constructed with individual letters from a Scale Link etched brass fret. Though slightly larger than in reality, they still do capture the look.

NZ Rifle Brigade uniform regulations were different from other NZ regiments, with blackened brass badges and buttons. These were represented with four different types of acrylic paint – a yellow base coat, then two blackening ink washes, and finished with stippled bright brass colour to mimic a weathered and chipped effect.

Other brass webbing fittings and buckles would have been tarnished and weathered, quite dull and definitely without the glint of a parade-yard look, though some sheen is possible due to scratching and from rubbing against other items when in use. For example, dome brass buttons for the pistol, gas-mask haversack and ammo pouches are all brighter due to being frequently buffed when clipping and unclipping the equipment. For these, and to show this, an extra shimmer was added using a little Jo Sonja Pearl White mixed with VBrass and Sepia wash, then finally glazed with Satin Varnish.

Tip

Regular brush care is important, as stippling, applying Flat Base and building up paint is tough on brushes. Wash them often, and from time to time use Jo Sonja brush conditioner or similar to restore bristles.

Painting Pack and Webbing Textures

The plan here is not to replicate exact webbing detail, but instead to attempt to simulate the appearance of light bouncing off a woven, patterned surface. Build up layers of paint in a similar way over the webbing and pack surface by loading lighter tones on to the highlight areas and adding Umbers in shadow areas. Some shadowing is done with 'Filters' – these are focused area washes that gradually deepen colours.

Over a few painting sessions, build up colours with a progressive stippling of thinner and longer

Painting the Webbing, Pack and Equipment

Important Steps	Key Points
1. Prepare to paint the small pack	* The palette used is the same as for the uniform, except VKhaki Grey replaces VEnglish Uniform. * Again, Flat Base and Blending Medium are mixed directly into each colour. Also have a small pool of these two mixed together ready to dip your brush into as you are stippling. * Undercoat the pack with Carbon Black.
2. Apply the base texture with the first stippling pass	* Use VKhaki Grey on a well-frayed, wide flat sable (Pebeo ~7mm). * This larger brush lays in the first spots in a loose stippling action, as the base texture. * Use a more defined and intentional pattern to create the base for the canvas fabric weave effect. * The blending medium helps create soft texturing.
3. Paint the small pack ribbing	Use sharper-edged flat brushes (Style × 5 and 6) to do finer stippled lines to represent the ribbing effect.

(Continued)

Continued

Important Steps	Key Points
4. Paint the mug	* Paint a smooth coat of Humbrol Gloss White with Humbrol Midnight Blue. * Add colour to represent tea sediment with VSatin Varnish + Game Colour Smokey Ink, a rich, intense colour, out of the bottle, slightly glossy and versatile for washes.
5. Paint the army blanket	* Use an older, frayed, pointed brush in a dabbing pattern to smoothly mix each tone together: *Base*: Carbon Black *Shadows*: Raw Umber *Highlights*: Payne's Grey + Naples Yellow * Use a fine liner brush to carefully add thin lines of Napthol Crimson for the red cotton stitched border.
6. Paint the webbing	Webbing is meticulous work, forming ribs of weave one rib at a time, though it is painted in exactly the same way as on the small pack. *Undercoat*: Carbon Black *Base*: VGreen Ochre + VGreen Grey *Shadows*: Base + Raw Umber Second – Raw Umber + Carbon Black *Highlights*: Base + Naples Yellow
7. Paint the gas-mask bag	* The same palette is used as for the webbing, though painted with a smooth, worn canvas look. * Charlie's name stencilling was done with a fine pointed brush (Style × #1) based on an actual example (see Uniform Colours photos below) using Payne's Grey + Raw Umber.
8. Paint the leather – the pistol holster and the pouch	Citadel (C) acrylics tend to dry with a satin finish when worked repeatedly with a number of dabbed layers. The alternative for more sheen is to add either Satin Varnish to the paint during mixing, or add VGame Colour Smokey Ink as part of the painting process. *Undercoat*: Carbon Black *Base*: Gunze Cocoa Brown *Shadows*: Burnt Umber, CScorched Brown, CBestial Brown *Highlights and scratches*: CSnakebite Leather + Naples Yellow

horizontal paint strokes, the 'ribs of ribbing' mimicking light and dark sections of the webbing pattern. Remember also to add ground-in muck and dirt as you progress in building up the pattern.

Each texture effect is time-consuming and cannot be hurried. Patience is essential when texturing, and the intention is to achieve an overall scale effect, not duplication. Much of texturing is actually a stylized look and is over-exaggerated to trick the eyes into recalling the look of the actual material.

Painting Weapons

A prominent part of this bust is the well-sculpted Lewis gun. In this scale it is a huge 8in (20cm) long mini model in its own right. In order to show the full weapon it was decided not to cover any part of it, despite the fact that it was renowned for unreliability when dirty. Instead, consistent with Charlie and NZRB training, the Lewis has been recently wiped down, as soon as practical, so there is only minimal evidence of recent battlefield action, such as carbon build-up or dust and earth on working parts. After this quick clean, Charlie has taken shelter out of line for a quick fag before he heads back in. This fits with many good images of Lewis guns being carried without covers ready for use and at 'stand to' (this was when troops stood 'at the ready' at dawn and sunset when the risk of an attack was highest).

An alternative approach with the Lewis is to consider adding a temporary canvas or cloth cover over the bolt and feed mechanism, plus adding a barrel cover, or stuffing a suitable rag into the end of the barrel jacket to prevent soiling affecting the LMG's operation. This option is one to think about for any weapon, especially vulnerable platoon automatics.

A reference plate from Osprey's *New Zealand in World War I* has an illustration of the barrel jacket and magazine painted up in a khaki olive tone. Other photographs reinforce this practice, suggesting this was a way that soldiers chose to camouflage the most obvious part of the gun. It adds another nice little point of difference for our Dink, and can also be seen above on Harry's Lewis gun.

A large, older flat brush with splayed bristles was helpful in the first part of stippling shown on the small pack.

This dangling enamel mug was made from a Chapstick lid and was 'dirtied' with acrylic washes to indicate tea staining.

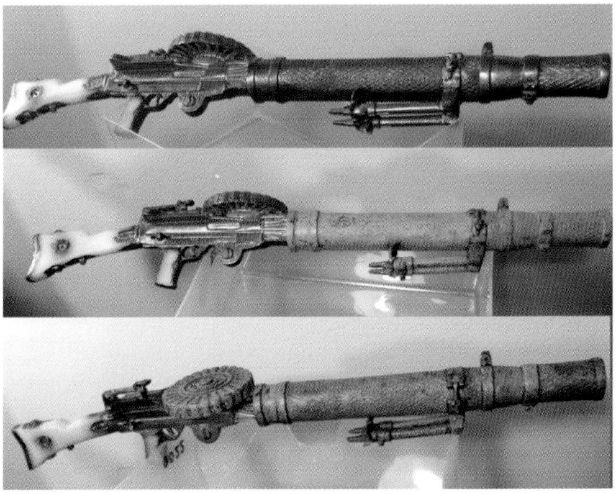

Stages of painting the Lewis gun: top: *polished lacquer;* middle: *jacket and bipod overpainted with acrylic;* bottom: *washed with oil paint.*

Painting Weapons

Important Steps	Key Points
1. Undercoat the Lewis gun	* VMatt Black – a couple of thin coats. * Mr Metals need to be a laid over a solid, complete base covering to be most effective.
2. Lacquer coat the metal surfaces	* Palette: Mr Metal Iron, Dark Iron, Aluminium, Stainless Steel. All can be mixed for added variety. * Use photos of an actual Lewis gun to see the different colours of metal parts on the real weapon. * Replicate each of these with a variety of Mr Metal Colour, such as Stainless Steel for lighter bolt area, Dark Iron for the main body, brass for the .303 ammo shell casings in the magazine. * Loosely flow on the Mr Metal layers, keeping them heavily thinned with natural methylated spirits. * Let one coat dry thoroughly for an hour or two before applying the next one. The longer you leave the pigment, the harder it will get.
3. Polish the metalwork	* To polish, use a soft nylon brush in a motor tool, a soft cloth such as chamois, and cotton-wool buds or swabs. * There are different polishing materials and methods, manual and powered; also allow for contrasting levels of sheen on metal parts. * Be careful to polish each painted section separately with a clean polisher to retain the different metal surface colours. It is possible to smudge or compromise colours that are next to each other or together – for example, if iron is buffed over brass the value of each colour will be lost. * Coat and polish over a couple of painting sessions, with more layers of Mr Metals gradually pooled over others (at least two to three for each section), and then polish. * Each consecutive polishing session increases the metal lustre.
4. Weather the metal-work	* For shadows and weathering use W&N Burnt Umber, Burnt Sienna, Lamp Black and Rowney Sepia oil paints, thinned with white spirits. Apply as focused pin washes, with the tip of a fine brush to emphasize joints, gaps and around raised detail like bolts, rivets and screws. * Use a finger or cotton swabs to smear oils over larger surfaces.
5. Overpaint the barrel and magazine	* Once satisfied with the metalwork, apply AK Interactive 'Worn Effects', or a similar product, over the barrel guard, bipod and magazine, then paint over these parts roughly with acrylic paint. Remember that in reality this painting would have been done under field conditions, and so makeshift painting materials would have been used. * Colour: CZambesi Desert – a semigloss sand shade, appropriate for paint on a metal surface. * This was a non-standard practice, so other colours are suitable, such as a lighter tan or dark green – the gunner would have used whatever was available, and whatever he thought would be the most effective camouflage – such as for painting helmets.
6. Overpaint the feed mechanism	* This area was coated with a protective satin black covering following surviving examples. * *Colour*: Apply thin coats of VBlack or W&N Ivory Black over the metal surfaces.

(Continued)

Continued

Important Steps	Key Points
7. Create wear on the overpainting	* When the barrel overpaint has dried, weathering can begin by remoistening this overcoat with Glaze Medium. * Rub, scratch and chip the painted surface with a toothpick or toothbrush to simulate battered paintwork. * Focus on those areas where paint would be more easily damaged when the Lewis gun is in use, such as the exposed end, underneath the barrel jacket, around the working parts and from the magazine changes.
8. Alternative way to wear overpainting	* For depicting damage and wear to minor paintwork a simpler alternative to using 'Worn Effects' is with a masking material such as Humbrol Maskol. * Apply the masking agent in random dots around the jacket, particularly at the barrel end and underneath. * Once the paint dries remove the Maskol with tweezers and Blu Tack. * Add extra scratching with a sharpened toothpick. * Be bold with wear effects as the Mr Metal is a strong base and difficult to remove once applied.
9. Weather the overpainted sections	* Again, leave component surfaces to dry, then apply thinned oils in pin washes and broader washing over the length of the barrel jacket. This will blend painted areas together. * Rub Lamp Black around the barrel jacket nose to represent carbon staining and residue from sustained firing. * Each area of the weapon was weathered separately to give the mixed appearance of different metal surfaces. * CZambesi Sand overpainted surfaces were finally touched up with fresh paint to highlight and emphasize edges of wear.
10. Paint the woodwork	* *Base* – VPanzer Ace Old Wood. * *Overcoat for wood grain*: W&N Burnt Umber, Burnt Sienna, Rowney Sepia. * The oils were not thinned, but instead were left sitting on a business card (or absorbent surface) for approximately 20 minutes, then used raw directly off the card. * Thin wood-grain patterns were painted on with a fine-pointed brush.
11. Paint the Webley pistol	* Exactly the same painting approach was used for the exposed section of the Webley pistol in its holster.

Tip

Use jeweller's awls for small circular details. These can easily punch out tiny rivets and buttons from soft metal foil (lead or pewter). Put a tiny dot of superglue on the new location, then pick up the foil rivet with the moistened end of a toothpick point.

Charlie is mounted on his display base with an actual Lewis gunner qualification badge and a NZRB collar badge.

Mammoth 1:6 busts allow for even more painting effects – a bruised, bloodied right fist, a muddied forearm and holster threading.

The bloodstained and torn cuff has been folded up to allow a field dressing to be applied to Charlie's weeping wrist injury.

Chapter Eight

Scratch-Building Figures and Busts

Simple Figure Conversions

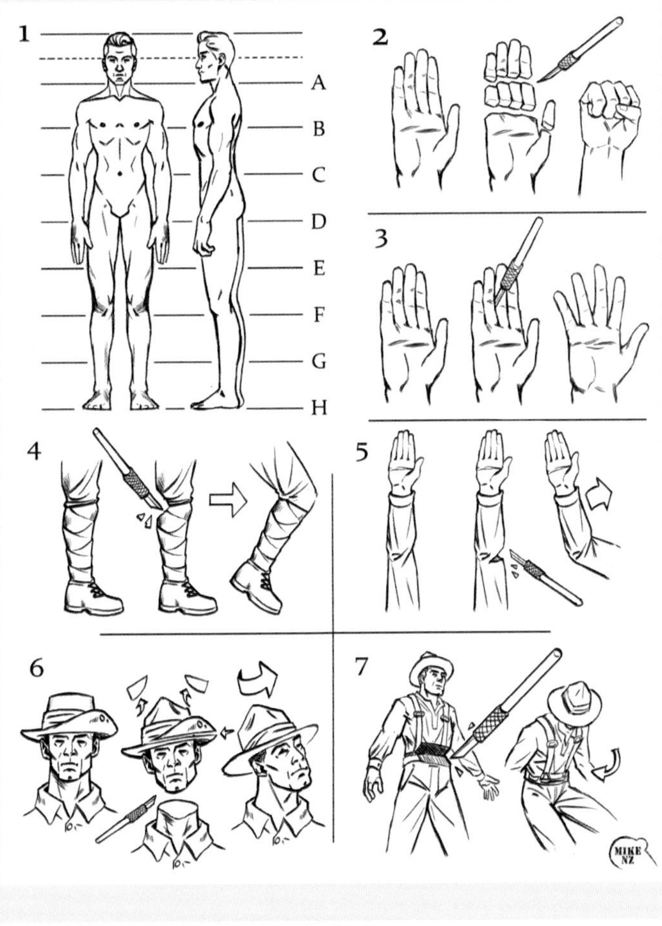

(Continued)

Continued

1. *Scale chart*: Use this chart to check that scaling is correct when converting or scratch building. Figures are typically measured as 'eight heads tall', starting from the top of the head:

   A – Tip of the chin – the eyes are located centrally on the head
   B – The nipple line
   C – The lower torso, with the belly button at the same height as the elbow
   D – The crotch, hip joints and wrist when the arms are at the side
   E – Stretched finger tips versus curled fingers
   F – Base of the knee caps
   G – Bottom of the calf muscles
   H – The soles of the feet on the floor or ground

Note: *See* the modelling armature kits and spares photo later in this chapter:

   * These armatures come in slightly different forms and are all generally based on this scale-chart approach.
   * Parts are provided for the head, upper and lower torsos, hands and feet or boots.
   * These parts are either joined by etched parts or by adding lengths of soft wire to pose.
   * Wire is then coated with putty – *see* Phil Walden's novel idea of adding thread to give putty a surface to key into.
2. A flat hand or poorly sculpted hand can be made to grip with a couple of simple modifications:
   * Cut or remove wedges from two finger joints and one thumb joint.
   * Carefully fold the finger section into a fist or around the handle, rifle fore grip or shaft.
   * Glue and fill the detail with epoxy putty.
3. Whenever you are faced with an outstretched hand:
   * Take time to separate and spread the fingers apart for a realistic look.
   * Even a couple of side fingers or a thumb apart from other fingers is more realistic, especially if these are not gripping an object.
   * Use a new scalpel blade tip to remove material between each finger.
   * If plastic or resin, dunk in hot water to slightly soften each hand and fingers.
   * Carefully separate and ply the fingers apart.
   * An alternative approach, or if a finger breaks, is to remove the kit fingers, drill into the hand, glue in lengths of brass or fuse wire, and finish the fingers with putty.
4. Change the straight leg to a bent leg for a running or walking pose:
   * Remove the wedge at the back of the knee.
   * Reposition the leg, glue in place, and fill the gap with putty.
   * Consider also changing the foot angle by removing a wedge at the front of the ankle.
5. Change the straight arm to a bent arm:
   * Remove the wedge at the inside of the elbow or wrist.
   * Reposition the arm and hand, glue in place, and fill the gap with putty.
   * Reverse the process if straightening out an arm.
6. Turn the head or change the headdress:
   * Remove the head and headdress.
   * Remove the wedge at the base of the neck; it can be filled for looking, or closed if looking down.
   * Remove unnecessary parts of the hat, then rebuild and reshape with putty.
   * Reposition the head, glue in place, and fill the gap with putty. Remember to keep the Adam's apple central when twisting the head.
7. Create a crouching or seated figure, done in the same way as with the limbs:
   * Remove a wedge from the front of the waist.
   * Lean the torso forwards, glue, then fill the gap.

Tip: Before fixing a pose in place, use Blu Tack to temporarily fix the parts. Then test and compare any new posing with photos or artist sketches to ensure it is anatomically possible.

PHIL WALDEN – MASTER SCULPTOR

Phil Walden is an internationally renowned World War I figure sculptor and modeller. He has brought a genuine sense of passion and artistry to his miniature art for almost forty years. Phil learnt his foundational skills, and gained an understanding of artistic design, through his professional trade as a traditional sign writer. Though Phil has recreated dramatic action poses, he specializes in casually posed figures, requiring a good understanding of how the human body relaxes when tired and worn out. These are further inspired by the art of famous Australian war artist Ivor Hele, who captured the sense of soldiers at rest and in combat. Phil recommends Hele's art as a primary source for figure sculptors and modellers.

Phil chooses to work in larger scales of 120mm (1:16) to 150mm (1:12). Photographs and explanations using Phil's figures are included here as examples of basic assembly and kit construction, plus conversions of existing kits and custom builds, also original one-off sculptures that he is best known for. Phil has few equals in original, large-scale World War I subjects, therefore his body of artwork provides an ideal example for us all to study and learn from.

Phil's most powerful representation of Gallipoli action has this young Fernleaf infantryman captured in the agony of his final moment.

The full pathos of this soldier can be seen, with the fatal wound delicately suggested by spattered blood on his cap cloth and shirt.

Phil Walden's Approach to Sculpture

Each of Phil's projects starts with design sketches, then shaping a rudimentary human form. He makes a basic armature, crafted from a simple wire frame, to get the initial pose. This is supplemented where required with precast spare parts, such as boots or hands.

Once the body shape has been fixed, Phil uses thick cotton embroidery thread wound in layers around the arms and legs: the shape of the musculature will be built on this. Once happy with this, Phil locks the figure's position in place by soaking the thread with superglue. This simple skeleton may be further bulked out with polystyrene foam around the torso. It is completed with thin layers of epoxy putty, carefully layered, then sculpted

Phil does the occasional bust such as this Light Horse trooper, masterfully painted in acrylics by gold medal New Zealand miniaturist John Belcher.

...He looks as if he is racing across and off the base, an effect reinforced by details such as a flying water bottle, and a strap chopped by a bullet.

Phil's charging Aucklander shows the power of dramatic pose and action emphasized by the tight base design...

Tip

Lead foil is harder to find today. It can corrode over time if not well primed and painted. Pewter foil is a soft, malleable replacement item.

into the gentle shapes of clothing. Particular effort is made to ensure that clothing falls naturally, and is consistent with the type of material it was made of. The thin cotton shirts at Gallipoli had much more wrinkling than the heavier serge battledress of Western Front British uniforms, which had soft creasing folds. Finally weapons, equipment and finer detail is built using spares, lead foil, wire, plastic card or carved epoxy putty.

Phil has his own signature and unique approach to painting with oils, including talcum powder rubbed into paint to show gritty, grainy and grimy effects on clothes and skin. Oils provide a natural sheen for flesh areas, plus polished wood on weapons and equipment. Each example shown here allows us to see effects achieved both in pose, design and final finish. Phil's pieces tend to a more artistic look than more conventional and modern sculpting.

Phil continues to provide inspiration to many World War I modellers young and old, and is still active in his local Queensland Figure Society, tending to focus on ANZAC subjects. Updates on past and local projects can be found on Facebook in 'Phil Walden Art Showcase': https://m.facebook.com/groups/488240207854618/

Captain Philip Henry Fry

Captain Fry was a highly respected West Australian officer in the 10th Light Horse, Australian Imperial Forces (AIF), who served in Gallipoli in 1915. He was mortally wounded on Hill 60 when he tried to return a Turkish bomb. His portrait is

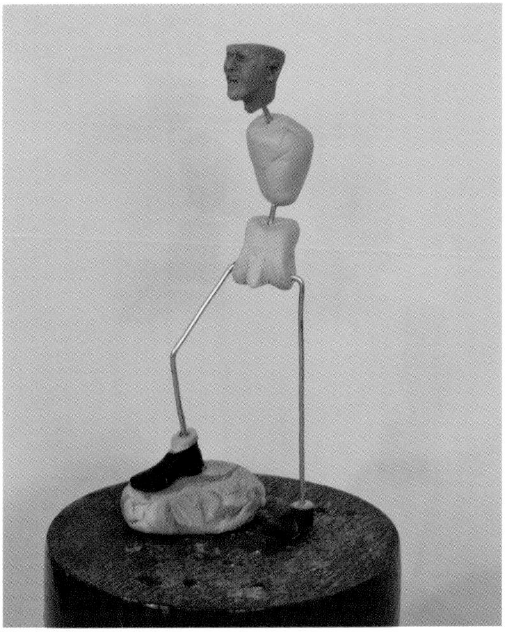

Phil uses a basic wire frame with a spare head, boots and roughly shaped putty blocks to form the torso body with hips.

Phil's classic ANZAC, showing a tired, wary man resting on the scrubby landscape, was sculpted late in the 1980s using his frame and cotton approach.

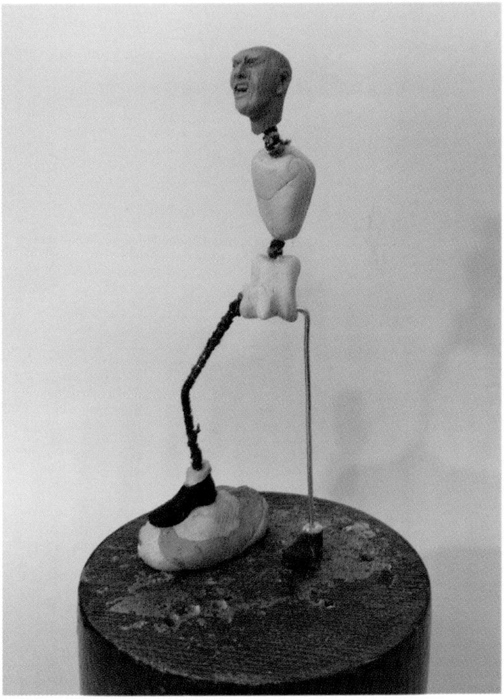

The wire frame is wrapped with embroidery thread, then soaked with superglue, giving a key for putty and still allowing for adjustments.

Academy armature figures, spare head and handsets are all useful starters for creating your own figures or converting existing figures.

An important part of suggesting movement is by using tape to show the loose webbing ends and bayonet frog flapping out from the body.

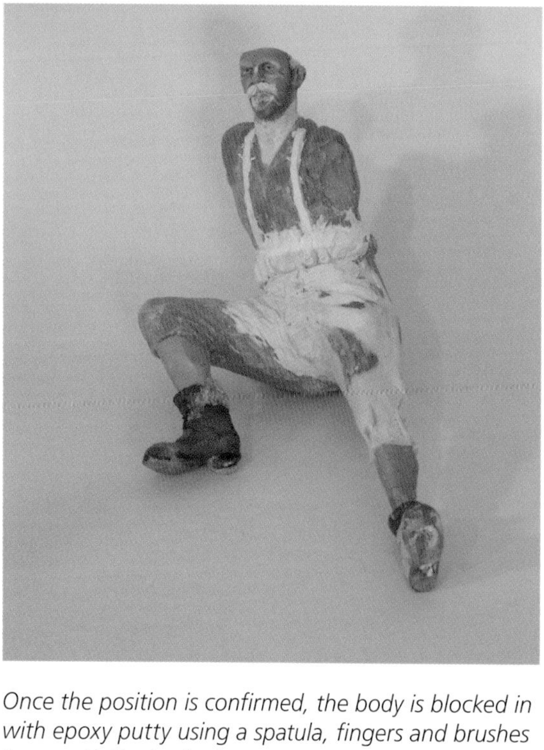

Once the position is confirmed, the body is blocked in with epoxy putty using a spatula, fingers and brushes to smooth the body shape.

The '1915' proposed composition brings together three figures, connecting the jigsaw puzzle of their poses into their final assault on Chunuk Bair or Hill 60.

synonymous with the look of an officer on the Peninsula at this time: weary, dirty, scruffily dressed, yet alert and ready. Phil Walden was inspired by a famous photograph, showing the Captain leaning against a trench wall on either Russell Hill or Walker's Ridge, *circa* July 1915. A simple yet evocative pose hinting at the hot and dusty terrain in the height of summer.

Phil's one-off 120mm figure was partly undercoated by him to check the sculpting. The intention now is to refurbish and finish the figure. This will be done by adding missing detail seen in the final photo of Fry – a breast pocket full of letters, lanyards for pistol and compass, and binoculars (see Historical Note below). He stands in a dirty trench line, flies buzzing around and settling on him. Phil Walden added a unique artistic feature to the reverse of the figure's display base, an area usually left blank by modellers: he opted to paint a sketch of the rough, scrubby hillside of Gaba Tepe. It is an important aspect of this custom sculpture, and will be retained in the final version as an acknowledgement of Phil's artistry.

Captain Phil Fry in progress: an original miniature based on an iconic photo of him shortly before he was killed in action.

Reverse views: Phil Walden's partly completed Light Horse captain, with an autographed illustration of the heights above ANZAC cove.

Historical Note

Optical equipment was in short supply during the Great War. A national campaign called 'The Field Glass Fund' was conducted by the National Service League, asking for donations of binoculars and telescopes from sporting shooters, hunters and the public. These were collected for use by the British and Colonial units for reconnaissance and sniping. Each item was catalogued and stamped to show they were on loan. Post-war many were returned to their original owners. Tragically Lord Roberts, who sponsored this fund, died unexpectedly early in the war, and it was left to his widow and daughter to continue this charitable work.

SOURCE: The Great War Forum

PAINTING AND MODELLING A PHIL WALDEN WORLD WAR I FIGURE

The figure for this project is a New Zealand mounted rifleman in Palestine, 1917–18. Australian Graham McNamara shared his project notes for this figure.

This is another original one-off sculpt, with fine copper wire added as a cord for the pistol lanyard. The first step is undercoat painting with Tamiya fine primer. Then he airbrushes a Tamiya NATO Black coat, followed by a fine mist of Tamiya Flat White from a 45-degree angle above. This helps give a guide to the light and shade on the figure. Graham finds airbrushing the Tamiya colours helps the Vallejo/Jo Sonja acrylics flow really well across the surface, and also aids with the overall matt finish. (A good shortcut without an airbrush is to use the Humbrol acrylic rattle cans, first Matt Black, then a few quick passes of the Matt White.)

All flesh areas were painted with Matisse artist acrylics, which are slightly satin and give a great depth to flesh colours. The rest of the kit was painted with a combination of Vallejo and Jo Sonja acrylics. He finds mixing the two gives a great dead flat finish to the surface.

The base colour for the shirt was Vallejo Japanese Tank Crew Highlights + Jo Sonja Smoked Pearl. The breeches were painted with Vallejo English Uniform + Jo Sonja Provincial Beige.

All leather parts were painted using Scale75's Wood and Leather Paint set. Graham made sure to give the boots and leggings a dustier appearance as they would have been from dragging in the dirt. One tip he noted for painting leather parts in acrylics, is these can look too 'dried out' in appearance, lacking the slightly satin look compared with dead flat cloth. So after painting is complete, he adds a thin wash from Secret Weapon Miniatures called 'Baby Poop' (probably the most accurate colour description of any paint wash on the market). This gives leather parts a slight satin sheen.

Graham also channelled a Steampunk effect in the painting of the goggles and telescope using Darkstar Miniature Molten Metal range of paints. Finally for that touch of extra detail he painted grid squares and basic detail on the reverse of the map.

Finally Graham McNamara says: 'Hopefully I've given life to a great sculpt from the master.'

Graham primes the original sculpt with a grey undercoat, then black and white overspraying in a form of pre-shading and pre-highlights.

Flesh and clothing have been completed, leather base tones blocked in, and evidence of black/white undercoat misting on goggles, boots and base.

Phil Walden's natural sculpture style can be seen in this New Zealand mounted rifleman finished in acrylics by fellow Queensland modeller Graham McNamara.

On the back, note details such as the water-bottle strap added from Tamiya tape, the unbuttoned back pocket, and the fine grid markings painted on the map.

Chapter Nine

Modelling a Diorama

Kia mate ururoa, Kei mate wheke.
(Fight like a shark, not like an octopus.)
Maori Whakatauki (proverb) for bravery

Author's Note

This small scene was inspired by the memoir of 16/256 Private Rikihana Carkeek, 'Home Little Maori Home' in which he shared his story as a member of the short-lived New Zealand Native Contingent in Gallipoli in 1915. It contains three converted 1:32 Tommy's War figures, and is intended as a small tribute to ANZAC units who served at No. 1 Outpost 'Maori Pah'.

Four life stories are threaded together through this small scene. Rikihana 'Bunny' was twenty-five years old, the same age as Trooper 'Ed' Jackson, of the Wellington Mounted Rifles. Their paths would cross with my great-uncle Edward Flaherty on Chunuk Bair during the August offensive. Ed was killed in action as the Turkish troops reclaimed the heights. Bunny and my relative were both badly wounded, with each being officially listed as casualties in the *Christchurch Sun* on 5 September 1915. Captain Peter Buck (Te Rangi Hīroa) was the medical officer assigned to the Native Contingent, and would have treated the injured from the Chunuk Bair battle.

New Zealand Maori troops arrived in early July 1915 with the aim of providing labouring and pioneering support, plus reinforcements to line operations. This vignette began a number of years ago as a simple grouping of three New Zealand conversions of Tommy's War figures with replacement 1:32 Roger Saunders' heads. 'Ed' was a Wellington mounted trooper, veteran of two months' fighting on the slopes, responsible for issuing supplies; another was the young and newly arrived 'Rikihana', shovel in hand ready for digging; and the other was a Native Contingent officer 'Peter', directing where to begin digging.

After further research, and in collaboration with Andy Belsey, the story to be told in the scene was finalized. A temporary hut, typical of those seen on ANZAC Cove, helps frame this Fernleaf reunion (the 'Fern leaves' was a more common New Zealand nickname for their soldiers in World War I; this referenced their Silver Fern badges). These huts were all along the shoreline, and clung to the side of the escarpments that rose above the beach. They appeared to have been hastily built from a simple timber frame, with a corrugated iron roof as protection from the elements. All the huts also looked to be adorned with various soft coverings, either to keep out flies, dust or blistering sunlight, or simply just to dry out bedding and clothing after washing in the sea.

Progress to date on each conversion and the hut is detailed below to demonstrate how small scenes are designed, built and brought to life.

Rikihana and Ed as they appeared in 'New Zealand's Roll of Honour 1915', published by The Auckland Weekly News *Illustrated List.*

The figures are simple conversions with suitable replacement heads and posed in a triangular pattern so that they interact with each other.

Tip

Use blunt and broken-tipped scalpel blades to craft and cut partly cured putty or to create ragged tears in rolled putty sheets. The blade can be held and used just with fingers or in its handle.

It was surprising to find that the water's edge at ANZAC Cove is made up of multicoloured pebbles and stones.

Further up the Gallipoli beach it is sandy. Note how the disturbed sand is darker, as it would have appeared after landing troops had disturbed it with their footprints.

Painting Ed

Important Steps	Key Points (All paints Jo Sonja unless otherwise stated)
1. Paint the flesh	* Used Hornet head. *Base*: VBasic Skintone *Main*: Burnt Sienna, Raw Sienna, Cadmium Orange *Shadow*: Base + Burnt Umber, Payne's Grey *Highlight*: Base + VSunny Skintone, Plum Pink *Red tones*: VCadium Umber Red, Light Flesh Tint * All colours blended with W&N Blending Medium. * The hair on the arms is a visual representation done with fine crosshatching lines of light and shade, as Shep Paine's advice in his classic book *How to Build Dioramas*: 'Detail that you see is not fully discernible in its true form, and appears instead as a pattern of highlights and shadows.' * The risk therefore is that we leave out one or the other when trying to show detail. On this figure as much time was spent on the flesh highlights as on trying to depict hairy forearms.
2. Paint the shirt	*Base*: Payne's Grey *Shadow*: Raw Umber *Highlight*: Naples Yellow *Sweat*: Thin washes of base + Carbon Black * Flies were everywhere at Gallipoli. These were hinted at with tiny spots of acrylic Matt medium with VMatt Black.
3. Paint the hat	* The hat was replaced with a hollowed-out white metal felt hat from a spare Scale Link head. * Painted with AK WWI British Uniform Base, Light and Shadow set. * A square Puggaree badge was added to the left side with a small block of putty. Painted in diagonally halved black/white Wellington NZMR colours.
4. Paint the trousers	*Base*: VEnglish Uniform *Shadows*: Burnt Umber, Payne's Grey *Highlight*: AK British Uniform Light
5. Paint the boots	*Base*: Payne's Grey *Shadow*: Carbon Black *Highlight*: VGreen Ochre

Ed's pose implies that he has seen it all. He was inspired by Edward Jackson, killed on Sari Bair on 9 August 1915, only a year after he enlisted.

It was an honour to be given the opportunity to visit Gallipoli, and this project helped us to learn more about the campaign.

Ed's back shows his sweat-soaked shirt, ground-in dirt and the hated flies; on the left of his puggaree is the Wellington Mounted Rifles patch.

Painting Rikihana

Important Steps	Key Points (All paints Jo Sonja unless otherwise stated)
1. Paint the flesh	The head was a Verlinden 1:32 spare and a hollowed-out cap from the kit head. *Base*: Raw Sienna *Shadows*: * Hooker's Green + Alizarin Crimson * Base + Burnt Umber *Highlights*: Cadmium Red Light + Naples Yellow *Lips*: Burnt Sienna + Alizarin Crimson *Hair*: Base – Carbon Black + Skintone Base * All the above paints were blended with W&N Blending Medium and Satin Varnish.
2. Paint the uniform and cap	* All were painted using the AK Interactive WWI British Uniform set – Base, Shade and Light. * The proportions differed between each item – for example, more Light on the jacket and more Base on the trousers. *Alternative*: Vallejo paints *Base*: English Uniform *Light*: Green Ochre *Shade*: Chocolate Brown * Add Buff to the Base to vary the colour tones between the jacket, trousers, puttees and cap. * All were mixed with Tamiya X-21 Flat Base and W&N Blending Medium.
3. Paint the mug	The mug was painted with Humbrol enamels – Gloss white with an Oxford Blue rim. The bottom was stippled with oil Lamp Black, and the inside washed with Game Colour Sepia. * You can't have an enamel mug without it being used for all sorts. A fun touch is the charred bottom and the remnants of dinner or a brew still left in it – which was probably not as hygienic as these guys actually needed to be in order to avoid sickness.
4. Paint the boots	As Ed above.
5. Paint the shovel	The shovel was a spare accessory from an old US company, H&R, who made brass tools, with the T handle added from plastic rod and putty. *Blade*: Humbrol Gunmetal shaded with Lamp Black oils and dusted with VBuff *Handle*: Raw Sienna + VOld Wood
6. Paint the rifle	*Woodwork*: CDark Flesh *Shadow*: Payne's Grey *Highlight*: VNew Wood *Metal*: VGunmetal with Black and VPrussian Blue for shadows * A new sling was made from electrical insulation tape and fusewire buckles. The rifle was painted with VBuff + Raw Umber.

A young, pensive Rikihana glances in the direction indicated by his MO. Features include his mug, his cap sun flap, the tape rifle sling, and the tints of his jacket and trousers.

On his back Rikihana carries a pack, a covered mess tin, a waterbottle and a newly collected shovel for trenching and sap building.

Changes to the Peter Figure

Important Steps	Key Points
1. Replace the head and headers	* New Verlinden spare head was used as a base with a putty modification to the nose and features for a more distinctive profile. * A Scale Link white metal pith helmet was hollowed out using a motor tool, and the rim thinned out with careful sanding. A tiny badge was made from Magic Sculpt.
2. Change the boots	* The kit boots were cut off at just below the knee and replaced with a pair of putteed legs from another Tommy's War figure. * Superglued in place, then the joints filled with Apoxie putty.
3. Change the right hand position	* The fingers were separated, then a small wedge was taken out at the joints of each finger. * The fingers were straightened out and the gaps filled with superglue and Magic Sculpt putty.
4. Remove the binoculars and strap	* A sharp scalpel blade was used to carefully pare off the strapping. * Missing and damaged detail was replaced with Magic Sculpt.
5. Make the clipboard	* A square 7 [x] 9mm was cut from thin wood veneer. * A bulldog clip was fashioned from lead foil. * Cigarette paper was used for the notes on the board.

Captain Buck was 'Doc' – or 'tākuta' – for the Contingent. The boots on the original figure were replaced with putteed legs from another Tommy figure.

Spot the changes: the Native Contingent badge on the helmet, the right-hand fingers unfurled to make an indicating hand, and the left thumb rebuilt from wire and putty.

Although the Captain Buck figure has a long way to go, the early steps here help explain how minor changes can really make a difference.

Historical Note

Maori troops were known not only for their fearsome 'Haka' (war dance) near the front line, but also for their wry sense of humour. Here's an example from an October 1915 diary entry by a Maori soldier. He was commenting on senior officers meeting his unit after evacuation from Gallipoli to Lemnos:

> *A general wearing a monocle rode over; also saw an Admiral wearing one. The Padre wanted to know how it is the English get weak in only one eye.*

SOURCE: *Maori in the Great War* by James Cowan

BUILDING THE BACKGROUND – THE GALLIPOLI HUT

Author's Note

I am indebted to Andy Belsey for building the components and this diorama background for my figures. After several discussions on the composition of his diorama we used photos to determine the type of hut that he would construct. In the table below are his explanations on how he made the items, and the background to each. Also highly recommended is his book *Modelling World War I Trench Warfare* for more information on his creations.

Andy used images from an interactive, walk-through Gallipoli encampment called the 'Quinn's Post Experience'. He roughed out the concept using spare figures and a cardboard hut mock-up. These photos were used to discuss the size and shape of the base. Eventually we settled on an angled shed, thinner on the right side, allowing the newly arriving Maori to be walking into the scene from behind the hut. The other two figures stand in front of the hut, guiding the young Maori to collect equipment and where to go.

Building the Gallipoli Hut

Important Steps	Key Points
1. Design the scene	* Decide on the concept. * Sketch the components and composition. * Test out the layout using figures, with paper engineering for the main parts.
2. Cut and prepare the base board	* The base is cut from a thin sheet of high-density polyurethane. * The front edge is sanded to a slight incline. * The surface is covered with Polyfilla, then textured by stippling it with the fingers and an old brush.

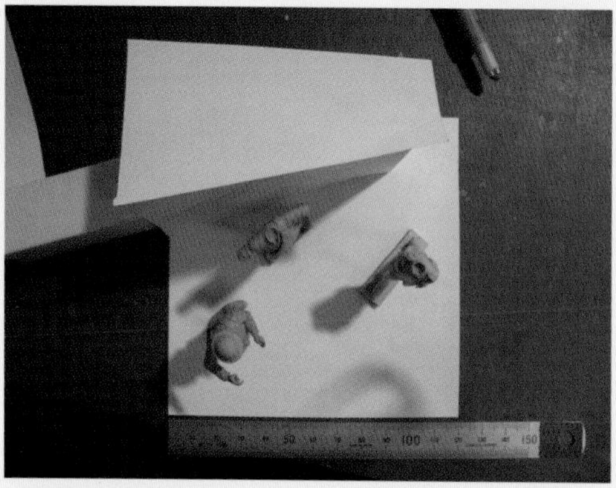

Andy mocked up the scene using paper and his spare Tommy's War figures, to help with design and sizing the vignette

Another rough layout with Andy's accessories and figures; one would later be converted into his map-reading officer 'Uncle' in the officers' dugout.

Important Steps	Key Points
3. Make the hut structure	* The wooden frame is cut from balsa. Planks for the sides are added. All the surfaces and edges are sanded smooth. * The back is cut from black styrene sheet to crop the back and sides of the hut. * The hut walls are glued to the base with PVA white glue, allowing for adjustment during the initial drying when any excess is easily removed from the black back board. * The plan is for the left side of the hut to be embedded in the side of the scrubby hillside. This will be painted and covered by real sand taken from the slopes around No.1 post.
4. Make the sandbag wall and top	* Small sausage shapes were rolled from Magic Sculpt, then chopped into about 25 × 11mm pellets; when filled these are about 5mm high and 20mm long. *Alternative option*: Fimo, or another oven baking clay, allows for finer-tuning before baking. * One end of the pellet is squashed down and squared to make the bag bottom. * The other end is pointed for the tied neck. *Alternative option*: Square off the bag top. Sandbags were not always tied, instead the bag opening was simply folded over. * Arrange the bags into rows with the tied end overlapping the bag in front. Make sure the bags bed well into each other.

(Continued)

Continued

Important Steps	Key Points
	* Add and shape a tab of putty to create the tied end. * Actual sandbags were made from a single folded section of hessian cloth with a sewn seam along the side. A seam was made on only one side of the bag by squeezing a ridge of putty with tweezers. * Vary the position of the bags with the exposed side seams, as not all sandbags were laid down the same way around. * Once dry, these seams and tops were thinned down with a sharp craft knife. * The sackcloth effect was lightly crosshatched into soft putty with the end of a pair of tweezers. * A filler paste of AK Modelling White Putty, mixed with hand lotion, was added around the sandbags to smooth them and fill the gaps between each.

Foil blankets and tarps hang down over an iron lid, held in place with a layer of sandbags to provide some protection from stray shrapnel.

Testing the final arrangement with the completed sandbag wall, shovels, 30lb biscuit boxes and water flimsies, including damaged ones thrown on to the roof.

Important Steps	Key Points
5. Make the hut roofing iron	Corrugated iron is the most utilitarian material used across generations of military housing. Gallipoli was no different, with stocks being shipped ashore early in the landing to go on to the myriad huts and holes the men bunked down in. * The sheets of iron are about 30 × 60mm in 1:32. * Andy uses a set of formers he has made to recreate sheets of iron from tinfoil pie dishes. The formers are two plastic card sheets, with lengths of 2mm plastic rod separated by 1mm square sections glued on top of them.

(Continued)

Continued

Important Steps	Key Points
	* Press the sheets of foil, cut to size, between the formers to shape the corrugations. **Note:** Corrugated iron does not readily rust due to its having a galvanized zinc coating; instead it goes a dull darker grey. Foil was lightly sanded and then dulled down with heavy coats of Humbrol Matt Cote.
6. Making soft furnishings – blankets and tarpaulins	Draped around all the huts clinging to the cliffs of ANZAC Cove was an assortment of blankets, tarps and washing. These were copied on the Quinn's Post Experience huts, with blankets hanging over the roof edges, adding interest and colour. * A number of folded blankets were made using pie-dish foil, which can be bent and burnished into hanging sheets. Sags in the cloth can be burnished into the foil. * Some edges have tassels, which were cut into the foil with a sharp scalpel. *Alternative option*: Epoxy putty was used to fill and add additional material. * Blankets were painted in acrylics as a mismatch of tartans and plain colours.
7. Assemble the roof	* The roof was given a final layer of sandbags for more protection from weather and shelling. * The roof iron and sandbags were superglued with SpecialT Ultragap filling CA to stick all the parts in place quickly. * White Apoxie Sculpt was used to fill and ensure a natural fit for the soft coverings protruding below the bags.
8. Make the boxes	The hut is intended as a pioneer quartermaster store, stacked inside and out with various stores ready for issuing. Andy manufactured a number of boxes and tools to decorate the scene. * Biscuit boxes were made from 10 × 12 × 17mm lumps of balsa. Two end panels were added with 0.5mm balsa to cover the end grain. Batons were also added to each end, made from 12mm lengths of 1 × 1.5mm balsa; panels were scribed into each side as if they had been made of smaller sheets of wood. * A fine 0.05mm ink pen was used to simulate the printed name for a prominent ration supplier – 'Walker, Harrison & Garthwaite' of London. *Note:* The aim for box printing was to show the shape of the text rather than each individual character. * Boxes were finished with thin oil-paint washes.
9. Make 'flimsies' – water cans	Reused petrol cans were one of the main containers used for transporting precious water on Gallipoli. These small 2-gallon tins were just the right size for troops to shuttle water back to their huts and trench line. Another common ANZAC water carrier was the milk and cream pail brought from home. * Flimsy cans are 8 × 5 × 9mm in 1:32. * Andy has made an art of producing these from tinfoil dishes and aluminium foil tape. This adhesive-backed tape is used to stick around foam cores. * Each core is lightly sanded with fine sandpaper before cutting into pieces. * Flimsy tops and bottoms are 8 × 5mm squares cut from aluminium tape and stuck to the core.

(*Continued*)

Continued

Important Steps	Key Points
	* Follow this by wrapping a length of 9mm tape round the foam core to form the sides. * Cut tinfoil strips 1 × 11mm to fold into the 5mm-long diagonal handles. * Superglue the handle made from tinfoil dish and a pouring spout made from a 2mm-high disc using 1.5mm plastic rod. * One nice thing about using foil is it is easily dented and damaged – *see* the old flimsy on the hut roof. * Roughen the foil with a light sanding before painting. * These were painted in a range of colours depending on the original fuel supplier and soon became scratched, chipped and dented in use.
10. Make the general service (GS) shovel	The main role of the Maori contingent on Gallipoli was as diggers* and pioneers. They had already shown their prowess in Malta, with a famous photo showing Peter Buck, with fellow officers, winning a trench-digging competition against British troops. The overall 1:32 length of the GS shovel is about 30mm. * Start with a 25mm shaft of plastic 1.5mm rod. * Cut a 4mm length of 1.2mm rod for the handle. * Superglue the handle on to one end of the shaft. * Cut an 8mm square from 0.5mm plastic card. * Then remove a 3mm deep socket in one end of the blade for gluing the shaft into. * Sand smooth all the connections when fully dried. * Crop the blade end for the rounded shovel, or square the spade end. Carefully bend each side to curve the blade. * Finish the top of the blade with a 0.5mm plastic strip, then smooth this into the blade and handle with putty. * **Historical Note:** The ANZAC nickname 'diggers' actually originated when associated with New Zealand trench diggers – Maori and Otago noncombatants on the Western Front in 1916.
11. Paint the basecoat	The painting process is begun with spray coats of Citadel Zandri Dust on the upper surfaces, and Chaos Black on the underside and inside of the hut. These are useful colours to seal the surfaces in readiness for painting textures and patterns on the various materials.
12. Make the other accessories	* 303 Ammo boxes are Scale Link white metal and etched brass accessories. * Barbed-wire reels are made from wood veneer and copper fuse wire. * Iron pickets for wiring are 20mm lengths, cut from Slaters angle-shape plastic rod, with two holes drilled in the top. * The broken wooden box on the roof is made from tan veneer, and 'damaged' with a sharp blade. * Rags on the ground and roof were made with thin epoxy putty.

Ed stands amongst Andy's handmade treasures. Some will be in the store hut, others piled outside ready for issue to new arrivals.

The painting process for the scene began with Citadel enamel spray coats; then lads and various accessories, including a 'Welcome' sign, are positioned.

Organized clutter helps to show the purpose of the hut for issuing various supplies and pioneering equipment, including barbed-wire reels, pickets, rations and water.

Water-based filler, mixed with hand lotion, was smeared round the sandbags to smooth the bags and fill the gaps between each layer.

Workbench set-up: optivisor, 3.5 x reading glasses, tools, putty and new brush-cleaning water trays made from a deodorant bottle holder.

The heights above ANZAC Cove reveal a tan sandy soil covered in scrubby plants and undergrowth used as cover by the attacking and defending soldiers.

Historical Note

The only drinking water we had was the water that came from Egypt in benzene tins. I think it must have been half petrol half water – that's what it tasted like, anyway.

Gallipoli Veteran

Invaluable detail for the Gallipoli scenes: 100 years on, poppies still bloom on the Chunuk Bair ridge line amongst other coloured flowers and shrubs.

The front view shows our three characters with an organized clutter of pioneering supplies around them. Each figure and item included helps to tell the overall story.

The side view details: patterned and Army-issue blankets plus rubbish and rags made from epoxy putty on roof and ground. All colours blend with groundwork earth.

Making Cloth, Rags and Sheeting with Putty

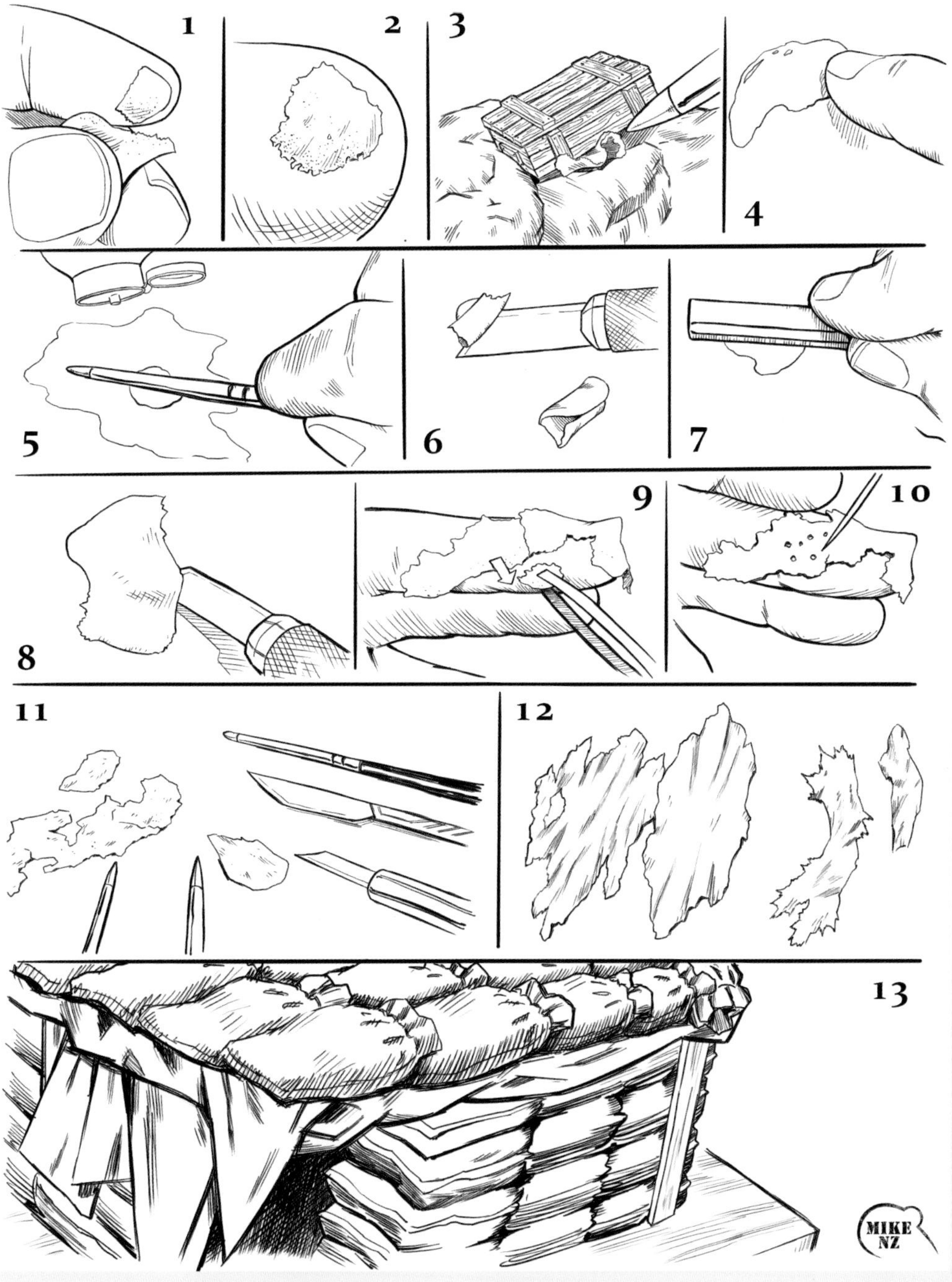

(Continued)

Continued

* As epoxy putty starts to cure it can be squished between the fingers into thin sheets that are almost transparent.
* Edges can be lacerated by softly tearing the sheet.
* Small pieces of sheet can be added as frayed cloth scraps, for example as debris from explosions. Use a rubber brush to push these naturally into crevices or gaps.
* Smooth out the sheets with a finger for a texture effect.
* An alternative is to roll out smaller flat sheets using the ferrule of a rubber brush. Be sure to cover the surface and rolling tools with a thin coating of hand lotion to prevent the putty sticking to surfaces.
* Create rolled sheets, such as maps or newspaper tubes, by curling small putty sections as you remove them from the surface with a blade.
* Rub larger sheets smooth with a modelling knife handle. Larger rollers such as these handles, or a small piece of dowel, can create bigger pieces of cloth too. Also, add effects from the roller surface – for example the knurled side of a handle or the wood grain of a dowel.
* Pry large sheets up with a sharp blade.
* Large pieces can be positioned, pulled and ripped with tweezers.
* Holes can be easily created using a sharpened toothpick. A broken toothpick dipped in hand cream also helps to push putty into place and add rough tatters.
* Make rags from putty, with tools (rubber shapers, blunt and sharp blades) used to shape, position and damage or cut thinned epoxy.
* Once flattened out, putty sheets can be easily creased, torn and folded naturally. Do leave putty to cure a little longer before putting into final position on figures or into scenes as sheeting or tarpaulins.

Chapter Ten

Closing Reflections

CLOSING REFLECTIONS

The Value of Shared Learning

Writing and publishing articles on different projects over the years forced me to reflect on how I paint. This sharing also encouraged me to become more systematic with my approach to painting, so it can be described for others. Others have said that I now have a recognizable style, especially in the character of faces and texturing. Together these show an authentic feel for the common fighting man. So do grab opportunities to share your projects with others, as the community support and critique from modelling peers will help maintain enthusiasm in the hobby.

A friend once asked 'How big are your figures?' I started taking 'pea portraits' of work-in-progress projects. Always be creative and enjoy what you do.

TIP

Experimenting gives us a chance to challenge the way we think about how we paint, and helps us to learn purposefully and to avoid becoming stale.

The Value of Experimentation

You will note that throughout the book I continue to experiment with a range of tools, colours and paint sets to allow each figure project to vary slightly as I learn. All of this is intended to help keep projects fresh, while learning to be more efficient with each practice.

The Value of World War I Modelling

I trust this book has shown that whether it be flesh, or uniform colours such as Khaki and Bleu Horizon, this World War I period is not dull or boring. Each figure or bust offers different approaches, colouring and texturing to capture these uniform colours. Rather than adopting a formulaic approach, the intention here has been to show how the hobby can begin with basic colours. Extending and varying these, one can learn many techniques to represent the soldiers and environments of World War I more effectively.

O'Flaherty doesn't look impressed. Thumbs up after completion of the Carl Reid sculpted ModelCellar 1:9 bust as a Lewis gunner of the 1st Royal Munster Fusiliers.

The Value of Looking Forward to What's Next...

I've tried to open the mind for the potential possibilities of World War I modelling, and I look forward to covering many more projects. Consider all the other options below and have a go!

* Cavalry, tunnellers, signalmen, despatch riders, nurses, doctors, YMCA and women's service units.
* Remember the contribution of animals: horses, camels, pigeons, dogs, donkeys and mules.
* Other allies and Arms of Service: Canadians, US Troops, Highlanders, sailors, desert pilots, French Colonial Africans, Asian pioneers and Arab auxiliaries, Italians, tankmen, air forces, armoured-car units of other allies such as Russia, Portugal, France – the list just goes on and on...

There are also bound to be many other tempting offerings coming from innovative manufacturers, or you can create or convert your own.

GALLERY

This section covers other topics and finished World War I projects.

It is exciting working with a new World War I figure maker, on the bench soon, Jean-Luc Frey's 'Wars & Peaces Miniatures'. ANZAC and dummy sculpted by Benoit Cauchies.

Women in Service

There are not enough female figures from the era, but hopefully this will change in the years to come when their sacrifice is fully appreciated. Only a few manufacturers have released kits, including Tommy's War – Nurse and Signaller. Women played a vital role in the Allied effort by backing up front-line soldiers as ambulance drivers, despatch riders, nurses, doctors and signal operators – not to mention on the Home Front in munitions factories – the 'Canary Girls' – and other domestic support roles such as mechanics, clerks and truck drivers. There are few examples of women in action, however the Russians had some units including the legendary '1st Russian Women's Battalion of Death' – surely an opportunity for future projects?

Author's Note

It was not possible to cover all nations or other projects within this book, as I did not have high resolution step-by-step photos. However, sharing a few further completed examples with additional background information may help when tackling other World War I subjects.

Tommy's War 'Gwen' – a Signals Sergeant in France 1916. A petit sculpture by Benoit Cauchies with the blue stripes of Queen Mary's Women's Auxiliary Army Corps.

Tommy's War 'Vera' – Benoit Cauchies sculpted this little nurse, which has been highly popular for hospital and aid-post scenes.

Painting women figures only varies from other figures in that more attention should be given to flesh tones, which should be softer and pinker with less shadowing or blue zone effects.

The Italian Front – Alps Reaching to the Sky

The conflict in Italy is also not well served with figures, and deserves more attention to be given some of the more interesting elements of it. Fighting was as intense as the Western Front in the main battles, and even more so in the Dolomites. This mountain campaign was awe-inspiring due to the conditions it was fought in. Beside Alpini troops, an interesting option are the Arditi Shock troops, looking like medieval soldiers. Other figure projects can cover all aspects of air and land battles. CSM added aircraft and Lancia armoured cars, so crew figures for these should also be on the horizon. For figure projects have a look at Allarmi, CSM, ModelCellar, MMA and ICM/Italeri.

Featured here is pioneering Italian aviator Francesco Baracca – his aircraft emblem was the rearing horse, which later became the famous symbol of Ferrari. A bank of photos of the original uniform was available for this project, and was invaluable to help achieve the colour tone, with authentic textures. The palette was as follows:

* AK Interactive WWI German Uniform Base + JS Payne's Grey
* *Shadow tones*: JS Payne's Grey + Burnt Umber
* *Highlight*: WWI French Uniform Light + Payne's Grey again help to tone it down.

Note: Regarding Payne's Grey I often use one 'core' colour throughout a figure to give an overall complementary effect.

The Russian Front 1914–20

World War I on the Russian Front, before and during the Revolution, has many options for interesting and intriguing figure displays. Not only

Francesco Baracca, the famous Italian ace painted for Copper State Models and intended to be paired with their Nieuport 17, sporting his prancing stallion.

Russian Imperial Automobile MG crewmen by Copper State Models – 1:35 figures posed together in a forested area created from real wood, foliage and ground scatter.

'Cecil' and 'Sid', RNAS armoured-car officer and driver grab a roadside brew while serving on the Russian steppes. Copper State Models 1:35.

'Ginge', in a white sailor's cap, and 'Bert', a petty officer in a navy-blue greatcoat, exchange glances while taking a break in Southern Russia.

were the various factions of Russians involved, but also other Allies contributed dedicated units for service there, such as armoured-car units from Britain and Belgium. Uniforms were very diverse, with a vast array of different Russian units, each with their own personal identification badges and colours. Attached allies such as the Belgians adopted a blend of their own and local ranks to avoid confusion. Many figures are being released, especially from this region, depicting the armed forces on the front. Examples to check out would be those from CSM, ModelCellar, Yellow House Club, Castle Miniatures and ICM. Expect more to be released as this theatre grows in interest.

The Last Post...

Listen to IWM's *Voices of World War I* and watch the BBC series *Great War Interviews*: http://www.bbc.co.uk/iplayer/episode/p01tcxg0/the-great-war-interviews-1-frank-brent

The following quote is from a veteran at the World War I fiftieth anniversary:

> *They went on waiting in front of the memorial, on this turf so immaculately maintained by the War Graves Commission. Thiepval is the only place for miles where the flower beds don't have a sign telling the public not to walk on them.*
>
> *'They would be irrelevant here,' Mr Hoadley said. 'I think everyone understands what this earth cost. The only people who really know about it, are underneath. I think this anniversary will be the last. When it comes to 75 years, we'll all be dead too, and the Somme will seem as abstract as Waterloo.'*

SOURCE: http://somme1916.wordpress.com/2013/03/02/somme-50th-anniversary-veterans-return/

APPENDIX I

Suppliers

This is not an extensive range of suppliers of World War I figure modelling items, however each listed here has provided good service to the author and other associates.

Name	Products	Website
AC Models	75mm and 120mm resin figures and busts.	www.facebook.com/ACModelsNZ
Allarmi	Small range of Italian 54mm figures and accessories.	www.italiankits.it/allarmi.html
Aviatic	1:32 figures and accessories to support aircraft modelling.	www.aviattic.co.uk
Blitz and JMD	Artillery, accessories sets and JMD range of figures in 65mm and 1:35 resin.	https://blitz-kit.fr/en/1_gamme-jmd
BNA	Stockists of an extensive range of figures, kits, tools, paints and all things modelling.	www.bnamodelworld.com
Cix Models	Produce 1:32 motorcycle kits and riders suitable for World War I scenes.	https://cixmodels.com
Copper State Models	Growing range of 1:35 armoured cars, 1:32 air-craft multimedia kits and resin figures in both scales.	www.copperstatemodels.com
DDay	Range of World War I figures includes good sets of World War I Belgians with dog cart and ANZAC desert patrol.	www.ddayminiaturestudio.com
Dolman Miniatures	High-quality 3D sculpted resin busts and figures.	www.dolmanminiatures.com
El Greco	Specialist figure and accessories supplier.	www.elgrecominiatures.co.uk
Figurinitaly	High-quality 1:32, 1:35 and 1:24 (75mm) 3D modelled handsets.	Via El Greco or other distributors
Historex Agents	Long-serving distributor of figures and accessories including Historex scenic accessories.	www.historexagents.com
Hornet Models	Roger Saunders is the legendary sculptor of these 1:32 and 1:35 headsets plus spare hands.	www.hornetandwolf.com

Name	Products	Website
ICM	1:35 plastic injection-moulded kits and accessories.	https://icm.com.ua
Jon Smith Models	1:16, 1:32 and 1:35 figures and accessories. Especially good for spare parts from sets, plus best rats and rum jars on the market.	www.jonsmith-modellbau.com
Kellerkind	1:32 resin figures, scenics and accessories primarily aimed at aircraft modellers.	www.kellerkind-miniaturen.com
Last Cavalry	US distributor of figures, busts and modelling materials.	www.lastcavalry.com/
Masterbox	1:35 plastic injection-moulded kits and accessories.	www.mbltd.info
Metal Modeles	Classic 54mm range of white metal World War I figures.	https://ateliermaket.com/en/38-pietons-wwi?id_category=38&n=26
Milit Model	54mm resin with specific focus on Italian subjects.	www.facebook.com/militmodel
MMA	Range of 54mm resin with specific focus on Italian subjects.	No website: search for distributors like www.zinnfigur.com
ModelCellar	High-quality resin figures including an extensive range sculpted by Mike Good.	https://ModelCellar.com
Naked Army and Khaki Army	Large 150mm, 180mm and 1:6 Polystone resin figures and busts.	www.na-int.com www.khaki-army.com
OzMods	Sole suppliers of Phil Walden 120mm figures.	www.ozmods-kits.com
Reedees Miniatures	Specialist range for larger-scale miniature weapons and headsets.	https://sites.google.com/site/reedeesminiatures
Royal Models	Expanding range of figures and accessories in a wide range of scales.	www.royalmodel.eu
Scalelink	Extensive range of 1:32 white metal kits.	www.scalelink.co.uk
Scalelink Frets	Brass frets especially useful for barbed wire, scenics and small lettering.	www.scalelinkfretcetera.co.uk
SK Miniatures	Specialist figure and bust distributor.	www.skminiatures.co.uk
Tommy's War	Sole supplier of most popular World War I range of 1:32 figures, cavalry, scenics and accessories.	https://tommyswar.co.uk
Wars and Peaces Miniatures	Supplier of their own range of resin 65mm figures and accessories.	www.wars-and-peaces-miniatures.fr
Yellow House Club & WW Model Studio	Wide range of niche World War I subjects, kits and figures.	https://www.facebook.com/yellowhouseclub
Young Miniatures	1:9 resin busts.	www.young-miniatures.com

APPENDIX II

Research Resources

WEBSITES

Topic	Website
10th Essex Living History Group	www.10thessex.uk
Australia	www.lighthorse.org.au
Belgium	www.arquebusiers.be/armee-belge-photos.htm
British & Commonwealth Military Badge Forum	www.britishbadgeforum.com
Canada	www.canadiansoldiers.com
FigureMentors	https://figurementors.com Digital figure modelling and painting magazine with leading artists sharing their approaches and experiences
France	https://lagrandeguerre.1fr1.net
France	www.dessins1418.fr
Great War Forum	www.greatwarforum.org
Nga Tapawae trails	https://ngatapuwae.govt.nz The New Zealand government World War I centennial project we used to help guide us around Gallipoli
NZ Auckland Museum cenotaph	www.aucklandmuseum.com/war-memorial/online-cenotaph/ Records and personal files of New Zealand service personnel
New Zealand official history	https://nzhistory.govt.nz/war/first-world-war
PlanetFigure	www.planetfigure.com
Western Front Association	www.westernfrontassociation.com Also have an excellent historical magazine *Stand To* rich with fresh stories and in-depth information on existing topics

BOOKS AND REFERENCES

'ANZACs on Chunuk Bair, Gallipoli Campaign, August 1915': SMH *Figure Modelling* No. 20 and also *Theme Collection*: Vol 4. *WW1 Modelling*.
Other articles: *Figure Modelling* No. 5, No. 8, No. 11, No. 17, No. 18, and *Theme Collection* Vol. 6.

Arthur, Max, and the Imperial War Museum *Forgotten Voices of the Great War* (Ebury).

Austin, Lt Col W.S. Austin, *Official History of the New Zealand Rifle Brigade* http://nzetc.victoria.ac.nz/tm/

scholarly/tei-WH1-NZRi.html – Original official history from the 1920s, published by L.T. Watkins Ltd.

Bean, Captain Charles, AIF Official War Correspondent, editor, *The Gallipoli Book* – content by serving soldiers on the Peninsula.

Belsey, Andy, *Modelling World War I Trench Warfare* (The Crowood Press Ltd).

Butler, Mike 'The Kiwi', *Developing Your Own Style #1 and #2: The Illustrated Historical Artist* Issue 8 and Issue 9.

Butler, Mike 'The Kiwi', *Mr Black's 'Scale Model Handbook'* (SMH) series (www.mrblackpublications.com).

FitzSimons, Peter: 1 *Gallipoli*
2 *Fromelles & Pozieres*
3 *Monash's Masterpiece*
4 *Victory of Villers-Bretonneux* (ABC Audio).

Fosten, Bryan, *Stan Catchpol's Modelling Workshop* (Military Modelling MAP).

Funcken, Liliane and Fred *L'Uniforme et Les Armes des Soldats de la Guerre 1914–18*: Part 1 & Part 2 (Casterman).

Gibbs, Philip, *Now It Can Be Told* (Audible).

Grey, John H., *From the Uttermost Ends of the Earth – The New Zealand Division on the Western Front 1916–18* (Willsonscott).

Harper, Glyn, *Johnny Enzed: The New Zealand Soldier in the First World War 1914–18* (Exisle).

Holmes, Professor Richard, *Tommy – The British Soldier on the Western Front 1914–1918* (Harper).

Jouineau, André, [Volume 1] *Officers and Soldiers of the French Army 1914: August–December 1914*.
[Volume 2] *Officers and Soldiers of the French Army 1918: 1915 to Victory*. (Histoire & Collections).

Lang, Dr Sean, *First World War for Dummies* (Wiley Audio).

Lerneux, Dr Pierre, *Die Belgische Armee im Ersten Weltkrieg* (*The Belgian Army in the Great War, Vol. 1 and Vol. 2*) (Verlag Militaria).

Lynch, E.P.F. (edited by Will Davies) *Somme Mud – Experiences of an Infantryman in France 1916–19* (Bantam).

McGibbon, Ian, *New Zealand's Western Front Campaign* (Bateman).

Mirouze, Laurent, *World War I Infantry in Colour Photographs – Europa Militaria 03* (The Crowood Press Ltd).

Mollo, Andrew and Turner, Pierre, *Army Uniforms of World War I* (Blandford).

North, Jonathan, *Illustrated Encyclopaedia of Uniforms of World War I* (Lorenz Books).

O'Sullivan, Barry, O'Sullivan, Matthew, and Brehaut, Tristan, *New Zealand Army Personal Equipment 1910–1945* (Willsonscott).

O'Sullivan, Barry, O'Sullivan, Matthew, and Brehaut, Tristan, *New Zealand Army Uniforms and Clothing 1910–1945* (Willsonscott).

Paine, Sheperd, *Building and Painting Scale Figures* (Kulmbach).

Paine, Sheperd, *How to Build Dioramas* (Kulmbach).

Pedersen, Peter with Roberts, Chris, *ANZACS on the Western Front – Battlefield Guide* (Australian War Memorial).

Philips, Jock (ed.) with Harper, Philip and Susan, *Brothers in Arms – Gordon and Robin Harper in The Great War.*

Powell, William F., and Foster, Walter, *Colour Mixing Recipes for Portraits.*

Pugsley, Christopher, *Gallipoli – The New Zealand Story* (Libro International); book to support the television series: https://www.nzonscreen.com/title/gallipoli-the-new-zealand-story-1984

Sebag-Montefiore, Hugh, *Somme: Into the Breach* (Penguin Audio).

Soutar, Monty, *Maori in the First World War Whitiki! Whiti! Whiti! E!* (Bateman).

Stack, Wayne and Chappell, Mike, *New Zealand Expeditionary Force in WW1* (Osprey MAA473).

Stanley, Peter, *Die in Battle, Do not Despair: The Indians on Gallipoli 1915* (Helion).

Sumner, Ian, and Graham Turner, Graham, *ANZAC Infantryman 1914–15: Warrior 155* (Osprey).

Index